A New Owner's
Guide to
ENGLISH SPRINGER
SPANIELS

JG-114

Overleaf: An English Springer Spaniel adult and puppy.

Opposite page: An English Springer Spaniel owned by Jane Schwarz.

The Publisher wishes to acknowledge the following owners of the dogs in this book: Nick Campenelli, Doris Cunningham, Barbara Czarzasty, Drew DiDonato, The Fritz family, Terri Gainnetti, Fred Grazioso, Joanne Hass, Jennye Hansen, Gail Jackson, The Kichler family, The Kipe family, Kathy Kirk, Larry Libeu, Tracy Monahan, John and Colleen Nicholson, Art Perle, Jane Schwarz, Bruce A. Smith, Jennifer Sweet, Michael Turpen, Linda Whalen, Bernard Yirko, Debbie Youberg.

Photographers: Tara Darling, Isabelle Francais, Robert Pearcy, Art Perle, Vince Serbin, Robert Smith, Karen Taylor.

The author acknowledges the contribution of Judy Iby of the following Chapters: Sport of Purebred Dogs, Identification and Finding the Lost Dog, Traveling with Your Dog, Health Care, Behavior and Canine Communication.

The portrayal of canine pet products in this book is for general instructive value only; the appearance of such products does not necessarily constitute an endorsement by the authors, the publisher, or the owners of the dogs portrayed in this book.

Distributed in the UNITED STATES to the Pet Trade by T.F.H. Publications, Inc., One T.F.H. Plaza, Neptune City, NJ 07753; distributed in the UNITED STATES to the Bookstore and Library Trade by National Book Network, Inc. 4720 Boston Way, Lanham MD 20706; in CANADA to the Pet Trade by H & L Pet Supplies Inc., 27 Kingston Crescent, Kitchener, Ontario N2B 2T6; Rolf C. Hagen Inc., 3225 Sartelon St. Laurent-Montreal Quebec H4R 1E8; in CANADA to the Book Trade by Vanwell Publishing Ltd., 1 Northrup Crescent, St. Catharines, Ontario L2M 6P5 ; in ENGLAND by T.F.H. Publications, PO Box 15, Waterlooville PO7 6BQ; in AUSTRALIA AND THE SOUTH PACIFIC by T.F.H. (Australia), Pty. Ltd., Box 149, Brookvale 2100 N.S.W., Australia; in NEW ZEALAND by Brooklands Aquarium Ltd. 5 McGiven Drive, New Plymouth, RD1 New Zealand; in Japan by T.F.H. Publications, Japan—Jiro Tsuda, 10-12-3 Ohjidai, Sakura, Chiba 285, Japan; in SOUTH AFRICA by Lopis (Pty) Ltd., P.O. Box 39127, Booysens, 2016, Johannesburg, South Africa. Published by T.F.H. Publications, Inc.
MANUFACTURED IN THE
UNITED STATES OF AMERICA
BY T.F.H. PUBLICATIONS, INC.

A New Owner's Guide to ENGLISH SPRINGER SPANIELS

Art Perle

Contents

1997 Edition

The Springer's weather-proof coat makes him ideal for field hunting.

Springers love to jump and do well in agility competitions.

Springers are natural hunters and retrievers, both on land and water.

The Springer's loving and happy disposition make him the ideal family pet.

The Springer is a well-proportioned dog built for speed and endurance.

HISTORY of the English Springer Spaniel

All of the eight breeds of spaniel currently recognized by the American Kennel Club derived from centuries-old, similar looking and acting dogs once collectively called "spanyells." This reference goes as far back as the late 14th century. Dr. Johannes Caius, in his famous book, *English Dogges*, written more than 400 years ago, said, "The common sort of people call them by one general word, namely spaniells, as tho these kind of dogges came originally and first of all out of Spaine. The most part of the skynnes are white, and if they be marked with any spottes, they are commonly red, and somewhat great therewithall, the heares not growing in such thickness but that the mixture of them may easely be perceaved. Othersome of them be reddishe and blackishe, but of that sorte there be but a very few."

English Springer Spaniels are excellent companions whose devotion to man is legendary.

From *How to Raise and Train an English Springer Spaniel*, by Robert Gannon (T.F.H. Publications, 1982), we discover that:

"Before the day of the shotgun, birds and small animals were caught mainly by nets. It seems that wildlife was not so fearful of humans as it is today, for netting wasn't difficult at all. The hunter would let loose a trained hawk which, gliding across the sky, would frighten small birds and animals and cause them to hide. Then a Spaniel would sniff them out, crawl up to them as closely as possible and crouch down, allowing his master to throw a net over both dog and game.

All eight spaniel breeds recognized today share the same collective ancestry and heritage as hunting and working dogs.

It is claimed that whole coveys of partridge could be netted in this way.

"Later, hunters developed another technique. Using one of the larger Spaniels to crash through the underbrush and frighten the birds or animals into flight, they would set either a falcon or a Greyhound in pursuit of the game.

"Gradually, the smaller dogs, trained to crouch and sneak up on game, became known as 'Cocking Spaniels,' or 'Cock Flushers,' since they were particularly adept at locating woodcock. These were the dogs we now call 'Cockers.' The larger dogs, used to 'spring' game into the open, were called 'Springing Spaniels' or, today, 'Springers.'

"So successful at hunting were Spaniels, both large and small, that, oddly enough, their very skill made them unpopular with some French kings. Fearing that Spaniels would eliminate all game from the country, one king even outlawed the dogs.

Fortunately for the breed, however, everyone else loved them. Hunters applauded them for their first-class ability in the field. Ladies liked them because they were friendly and well-mannered in the parlor. The old and still current French proverb—'Love me, love my dog'—was based on the loyalty between Spaniel and master, and the dog was often mentioned in the works of early English writers. Shakespeare, for instance, in his 'Henry VIII,' wrote: *You play the Spaniel, And think with wagging of your tongue to win me.*

"for many centuries, Spaniels were called wither 'springing' or 'cocking' merely because of their size and training, whether or not they came from the same litter. It wasn't until 1892, in fact, when the Kennel Club (England) gave Cocker Spaniels a

The Springer Spaniel and the Cocker Spaniel are closely related, both bred for hunting and locating game.

separate classification, that they were finally recognized as a breed distinct from other Spaniels.

"Springers, however, had to wait another decade before they acquired sufficient strength and 'fixity of type' to gain a show place of their own. Sir Hugo FitzHerbert deserves credit for publicizing Springers in England. With the help of a few other devotees, he exhibited his famous

The noble English Springer Spaniel has a illustrious history, dating back to the late 14th century.

Tissington strain and won almost all prizes available.

"Meanwhile, English Springers were gaining popularity in the New World. In fact, in spite of its name, the breed can be considered as American as any of us, for, according to Howard Chapin's 'Dogs in Early New England,' these Spaniels came to

Spaniels were used to sneak up on birds in the field, flush them out into plain sight and retrieve them for their master, a feat they still accomplish today.

Plymouth on the first trip of the *Mayflower*.

"Around 1866, sportsmen who lived in New Jersey and worked in New York are said to have made a practice of shooting for an hour or two with their Springers in the marshes of New Jersey before ferrying across the Hudson River for a day of work."

SPRINGERS IN AMERICA

As all types of spaniels became popular in the United States, the American Spaniel Club was founded in 1880 to try to sort the different varieties. The most popular of the Spaniels was the Cocker Spaniel, which was already being extensively shown in conformation. The ASC set the maximum size limit for Cockers at 28 pounds; heavier dogs were considered Springers.

All types of spaniels became popular in the late 1800s, but the English Springer's unique qualities were not recognized as a separate breed by the AKC until 1919.

It wasn't until the 1920s that Springers began to really make their mark on American sportsmen and fanciers. Howard Stout Nielson of Darien, Connecticut, was an early and influential breeder. On Fisher's Island, in New York, Mr. Henry Ferguson established the Falcon Hill Kennels in 1924 and began breeding and working Springers in earnest. Mr. Ferguson was a charter member of the English Springer Spaniel Field Trial Association, the parent club of the breed (formed between 1924-27), and served as its Honorary President until 1959. The first Springer field trial in the U.S. was held on Fisher's Island.

Today's English Springer Spaniel retains his popularity with his sweet and loyal disposition and his reputation as a fine hunter and retriever.

In 1919, the first English Springer Spaniel was registered in the American Kennel Club Stud Book. She was Denne Lucy (#14264), bred in England and imported to the United States by Hobart Ames of North Easton, Massachusetts.

TODAY'S SPRINGERS

The English Springer Spaniel has maintained its popularity over the years, remaining one of the top 25 breeds registered with the American Kennel Club. He reached the height of his popularity when President George Bush and Mrs. Barbara Bush brought their Springer, Millie, to the White House. Millie was a regular at White House functions, and even bore a litter there. *Millie's Book*, as told to Barbara Bush, was a best-seller for a time.

In 1993, a Springer ascended to the top of the dog-show world by winning Best in Show at the prestigious Westminster Kennel Club show in Madison Square Garden in New York. He was Ch. Salilyn's Condor, owned by Donna S. and Roger H. Herzig, MD, and Julia Gasow, and handled by Mark Threlfall. Today, as always, the breed is loved for its sweet disposition, fine hunting ability, handsome looks, medium size and devotion to his owner. No wonder he's a popular dog.

STANDARD of the English Springer Spaniel

The English Springer Spaniel is listed in the American Kennel Club as a member of the Group I Sporting Dogs. He is bred for practical use as a hunter with the physical stamina to perform for hours under difficult conditions and to do so while under control at all times. He must also work with one or more gunners on land, marsh or water and on occasion handle rabbits or birds weighing eight to ten pounds. He should also conform to the standard for the English Springer Spaniel in type and quality for this purpose.

The Springer Spaniel is a hardy breed that possesses strong physical stamina and is able to work long hours in the field carrying heavy game.

For some reason, many field-trial oriented Springer Spaniel owners are of the opinion that the breed standard for type and quality does not apply to the field trial, or hunting Springer Spaniel. You will find this thinking reversed when talking to show Springer Spaniel owners and breeders. They appear to believe that breeding for "practical use, stamina and obedience" applies only to field and obedience trial breeders.

A standard is only a blueprint for the breed, an "ideal" breeders strive to accomplish. An "imperfect" English Springer Spaniel can still make a wonderful pet. This is the official standard of the English Springer Spaniel approved by the American Kennel Club on February 12, 1994.

OFFICIAL STANDARD OF THE ENGLISH SPRINGER SPANIEL
General Appearance–The English Springer Spaniel is a medium-sized sporting dog, with a compact body and a docked

The English Springer Spaniel is a medium-sized, well-proportioned dog with a moderately long coat that feathers on his legs, ears and chest.

tail. His coat is moderately long, with feathering on his legs, ears, chest and brisket. His pendulous ears, soft gentle expression, sturdy build and friendly wagging tail proclaim him unmistakably a member of the ancient family of Spaniels. He is above all a well-proportioned dog, free from exaggeration, nicely balanced in every part. His carriage is proud and upstanding, body deep, legs strong and muscular, with enough length to carry him with ease. Taken as a whole, the English Springer Spaniel suggests power, endurance and agility. He looks the part of a dog that can go, and keep going, under difficult hunting conditions. At his best, he is endowed with style, symmetry, balance and enthusiasm, and is every inch a sporting dog of distinct spaniel character, combining beauty and utility.

Size, Proportion, Substance—The Springer is built to cover rough ground with agility and reasonable speed. His structure suggests the capacity for endurance. He is to be kept to medium size. Ideal height at the shoulder for dogs is 20 inches; for bitches, it is 19 inches. Those more than one inch over or under the breed ideal are to be faulted. A 20 inch dog, well-proportioned and in good condition, will weigh approximately 50 pounds; a 19 inch bitch will weigh approximately 40 pounds. The length of the body (measured from point of shoulder to point of buttocks) is slightly greater than the height at the withers. The dog too long in body, especially when long in the loin, tires easily and lacks the compact outline characteristic of the breed. A dog too short in body for the length of his legs, a condition which destroys balance and restricts gait, is equally undesirable. A Springer with correct substance appears well-knit and sturdy with good bone, however, he is never coarse or ponderous.

The Springer is a compact dog, built for speed, agility and endurance.

The head of the Springer Spaniel is strong and impressive, and his expression is alert, kindly and trusting.

Head–The head is impressive without being heavy. Its beauty lies in a combination of strength and refinement. It is important that its size and proportion be in balance with the rest of the dog. Viewed in profile, the head appears approximately the same length as the neck and blends with the body in substance. The stop, eyebrows and chiseling of the bony structure around the eye sockets contribute to the Springer's beautiful and characteristic expression, which is alert, kindly and trusting. The **eyes**, more than any other feature, are the essence of the Springer's appeal. Correct size, shape, placement and color influence expression and attractiveness. The eyes are of medium size and oval in shape, set rather well-apart and fairly deep in their sockets. The color of iris harmonizes with the color of the coat, preferably dark hazel in the liver and white dogs and black or deep brown in the black and white dogs. Eyerims are fully pigmented and match the coat in color. Lids are tight with little or no haw showing. Eyes that are small, round or protruding, as well as eyes that are yellow or brassy in color,

The ideal Springer should have long, wide, hanging ears and a liver or brown nose, depending on his coat color. This is Rendition's Best Regards, owned by Linda Whalen.

are highly undesirable. **Ears** are long and fairly wide, hanging close to the cheeks with no tendency to stand up or out. The ear leather is thin and approximately long enough to reach the tip of the nose. Correct ear set is on a level with the eye and not too far back on the skull. The **skull** is medium-length and fairly broad, flat on top and slightly rounded at the sides and back. The occiput bone is inconspicuous. As the skull rises from the foreface, it makes a stop, divided by a groove, or fluting between the eyes. The groove disappears as it reaches the middle of the forehead. The amount of stop is moderate. It must not be a pronounced feature; rather it is a subtle rise where the muzzle joins the upper head. It is emphasized by the groove and by the position and shape of the eyebrows, which are well-developed. The muzzle is approximately the same length as the skull and one half the width of the skull. Viewed in profile, the toplines of the skull and muzzle lie in approximately parallel planes. The nasal bone is straight, with no inclination downward toward the tip of the nose, the latter giving an undesirable downfaced look. Neither is the nasal bone concave, resulting in a "dish-faced" profile; nor convex, giving the dog a Roman nose. The cheeks are flat, and the face is well-chiseled under the eye. **Jaws** are of sufficient length to allow the dogs to carry game easily: fairly square, lean and strong. The upper lips come down full and rather square to cover the line of the lower jaw, however, the lips are never pendulous or exaggerated. The **nose** is fully pigmented, liver or black in color, depending on the color of the coat. The nostrils are well-opened and broad. **Teeth** are strong, clean, of good size and ideally meet in a close scissors bite. An even bite or one or two incisors slightly out of line are minor faults. Undershot, overshot and wry jaws are serious faults and are to be severely penalized.

Your Springer's back and neck should blend together smoothly, suggesting length and muscularity.

Neck, Topline, Body—The **neck** is moderately long, muscular, clean and slightly arched at the crest. It blends gradually and smoothly into sloping shoulders. The portion of the topline from withers to tail is firm and slopes very gently. The body is short-coupled, strong and compact. The **chest** is deep, reaching the level of the elbows, with well-developed forechest; however, it is not so wide or round as to interfere with the action of the front legs. Ribs are fairly long, springing gradually to the middle of the body, then tapering as they approach the end of the ribbed section. The underline stays level with the elbows to a slight upcurve at the flank. The **back** is straight, strong and essentially level. Loins are strong, short and slightly arched. **Hips** are nicely rounded, blending smoothly into the hind legs. The croup slopes gently to the set of the tail, and tail-set follows the natural line of the croup. The **tail** is carried horizontally or slightly elevated and displays a characteristic lively, merry, action, particularly when the dog is on game. A clamped tail (indicating timidity or undependable temperament) is to be faulted, as is a tail carried at a right angle to the backline in Terrier fashion.

Forequarters—Efficient movement in front calls for proper forequarter assembly. The shoulder blades are flat and fairly close together at the tips, molding smoothly into the contour of the body. Ideally, when measured from the top of the withers to the point of the shoulder to elbow, the shoulder blade and upper arm are apparent equal length, forming an angle of nearly 90 degrees; this sets the front legs well under the body and places the elbows directly beneath the tips of the shoulder blades. Elbows lie close to the body. Forelegs are straight with the same degree of size continuing to the foot. Bone is strong, slightly flattened, not too round or too heavy. Pasterns are short, strong and slightly sloping, with no suggestion of weakness. Dewclaws are usually removed. Feet are round or slightly oval. They are compact and well-arched, of medium size with thick pads, and well-feathered between the toes.

Hindquarters—The Springer should be worked and shown in hard, muscular condition with well-developed hips and thighs. His whole rear assembly suggests strength and driving power. **Thighs** are broad and muscular. Stifle joints are strong. For functional efficiency, the angulation of the hindquarter is never the greater than that of the forequarter, and not appreciably less. The hock joints are somewhat rounded, not

The forequarters and hindquarters of your English Springer Spaniel should be equally proportioned and well-muscled for efficient, quick movement.

small and sharp in contour. Rear pasterns are short (about one-third the distance from the hip joint to the foot) and strong, with good bone. When viewed from behind, the rear pasterns are parallel. Dewclaws are usually removed. The feet are the same as in front, except that they are smaller and often more compact.

Your Springer Spaniel's tail is slightly elevated and should have a characteristic lively movement, especially when he is excited or on game.

Coat—The Springer has an outer coat and a undercoat. On the body, the outer coat is of medium length, flat or wavy, and is easily distinguishable from the undercoat, which is short, soft and dense. The quantity of undercoat is affected by climate and season. When in combination, outer coat and undercoat serve to make the dog substantially waterproof, weatherproof and thornproof. On ears, chest, legs and belly the

The Springer has both an undercoat and an outer coat, making him virtually weatherproof, waterproof, thorn proof and ideal for field hunting.

Springer is nicely furnished with a fringe of feathering of moderate length and heaviness. On the head, front of the forelegs, and below the hock joints on the front of the hind legs, the hair is short and fine. The coat has the clean, glossy, "live" appearance indicative of good health. It is legitimate to trim about the head, ears, neck, and feet, to remove dead undercoat, and to thin and shorten excess feathering as required to enhance a smart, functional appearance. The tail may be trimmed or well-fringed with wavy feathering. Above all, the appearance should be natural. Overtrimming, especially the body coat, or any chopped, barbered or artificial effect is to be penalized in the show ring, as is excessive feathering that destroys a clean outline desirable in a sporting dog. Correct quality and condition of coat is to take precedence over quantity of coat.

Your Springer's coat should look healthy and shiny. This black and white Springer owned by the Fritz family is an example of one of the acceptable coat colors.

Color—All the following combinations of colors and markings are equally acceptable: Black or liver with white markings or predominantly white with black or liver markings; blue or liver roan; tricolor: black and white or liver and white with tan markings, usually found on eyebrows, cheeks, inside of ears, and under the tail. Any white portion of the coat may be flecked with ticking. Off colors such as lemon, red or orange are not to place.

Gait—The final test of a Springer's conformation and soundness is proper movement. Balance is a prerequisite to good movement. The front and rear assemblies must be equivalent in angulation and muscular development for the gait to be smooth and effortless. Shoulders that are well laid-back to

A physically sound Springer will have a balanced, smooth and powerful gait.

permit a long stride are just as essential as the excellent rear quarters that provide driving power. Seen from the side, the Springer exhibits a long ground-covering stride and carries a firm back, with no tendency to dip, roach or roll from side to side. From the front, the legs swing forward in a free and easy manner. Elbows have free action from the shoulders, and the legs show no tendency to cross or interfere. From behind, the rear legs reach well under the body, following on a line with the forelegs. As speed increases, there is a natural tendency for the legs to converge toward a center line of travel. Movement faults include high-stepping, wasted motion; short, choppy stride; crabbing; and moving with the feet wide, the latter giving roll or swing to the body.

Temperament—The typical Springer is friendly, eager to please, quick to learn and willing to obey. Such traits are conducive to tractability, which is essential for appropriate handler control in the field. In the show ring, he should exhibit poise and attentiveness and permit himself to be examined by the judge without

The typical English Springer Spaniel is friendly and eager to please his master. Tee Dude and Sunny are owned by the author.

It must be remembered that the English Springer Spaniel is first and foremost a sporting dog, and this should always be reflected in his conformation and temperament.

resentment or cringing. Aggression towards people and aggression towards other dogs is not in keeping with a sporting dog character and purpose and is not acceptable. Excessive timidity, with due allowance for puppies and novice exhibits, is to be equally penalized.

Summary—In evaluating the English Springer Spaniel, the overall picture is a primary consideration. One should look for type, which includes general appearance and outline, and also for soundness, which includes movement and temperament. Inasmuch as the dog with a smooth easy gait must be reasonably sound and well-balanced, he is to be highly regarded, however, not to the extent of forgiving him for not looking like an English Springer Spaniel. An atypical dog, too short or long in leg length or foreign in head or expression, may move well, but he is not to be preferred over a good all-round specimen that has a minor fault in movement. It must be remembered that the English Springer Spaniel is first and foremost a sporting dog of the Spaniel family, and he must look, behave and move in character.

SELECTING Your English Springer Spaniel Puppy

The English Springer Spaniel has been trained to be a sporty hunting dog. Even if this is not the purpose for which you and thousands of others have selected your English Springer Spaniel, it is your duty to always keep this purpose in mind and allow this aspect of their personality to be expressed. It is their inbred birdiness, their eager desire to hunt, to retrieve, to accept training, to be of a tender mouth with a retrieve, to work with their handler, and to have a merry and loving disposition to other people and dogs that makes the English Springer Spaniel such a special breed.

The Springer Spaniel's loving and happy disposition and eagerness to obey make him a welcome addition to most families.

It is this loving, merry disposition, and desire to please that endears the Springer Spaniel to us. "Fawning like a spaniel" is a saying that goes back to the early history of the breed, and perfectly describes what is exemplified in the Springer: his love of people and of showing affection by leaping about, licking your hand, wagging his tail and otherwise indicating a desire to please all present.

There are many things you should consider before buying a dog. What is your reason for having a dog, especially an English Springer Spaniel? Will the dog be welcomed in your home by all members of your family? Who will be the primary caretaker of the dog? How much attention do you have to give to the dog? Not least of your considerations should be the size of the dog you choose in relation to your available space; the dog's need for daily exercise; the amount of food the dog will eat, the size of the area you can provide for the dog to relieve himself; housing the dog; and your ability to train the dog, possibly to become a hunting dog. You must do your homework and make a study of the type of English Springer Spaniel that will best suit you and your lifestyle.

It is best to see the sire of the litter you are considering, as well as the dam, and talk to the owner in order to gain additional information upon which to make your selection.

Many excellent bloodlines are available, and may be found either in the show blood lines or field blood lines. But unless you are intending to enter performance events or field trials, you may have a better selection for the all-purpose Springer Spaniel from the breeder who has owned and bred the same type Springer Spaniel as you wish to own. If you are looking for a dog that has suited all kinds of families for years, even for generations, you might choose the English Springer Spaniel that has been bred for the needs of the sport hunter, rather than a field trial-type Springer. Look at a lot of dogs and talk to a lot of Springer owners before deciding on what type you'd like.

CHOOSING A PUPPY

When going to look at puppies there are several things you should observe while at the sellers. Are the puppies, as well as the place in which they are housed, clean? Do they appear generally healthy and happy? Watch the dam closely as well and try to gauge her temperament. Is she friendly and responsive to her owners? Often, well-adjusted

Personalities vary within a litter, so choose a puppy that will fit your lifestyle. Sahdie Kipe poses with her Springer puppies.

Try to see the sire and the dam of the litter you are considering. Their overall health and temperament will help indicate what the puppies will be like.

puppies come from well-adjusted mothers. Also, observe the puppies playing together to determine the temperament and socialization skills of each one. Be sure to play with any puppy you are interested in away from his littermates.

English Springer Spaniel puppies may vary a little in appearance, and usually a litter will have a variety of sizes. As a normal selection, I would not take the largest or the smallest of the puppies, but any other that appears to be a suitable type. This means the puppy you choose should be without evidence of a poor bite, a deformed palate, eye problems, a protruding navel, deafness, a hidden or missing testicle, or a skin disease. Furthermore, ask the seller to sign an additional paper stating that he or she has no reason to believe the puppy or adult dog is anything but physically and temperamentally sound, with a full refund of the price if the animal is found to not be as it was represented. If the price is not too high, it might be wise to have the animal checked by a veterinarian for a small fee before purchase. The seller should be able to provide you with the necessary health credentials, pedigree and registration for the puppy you choose. You should feel free to ask any questions regarding the ancestors, health, training, grooming and temperament of the puppy you choose. If all of the facts indicate a healthy puppy or dog and you like him, there should be no reason not to take him.

It's hard to resist these adorable English Springer Spaniel puppies, but make sure that your decision to bring one home is a carefully considered one.

If you have not previously familiarized yourself with the certified pedigree of the American Kennel Club, you should write to them at 51 Madison Avenue, New York, New York 10010 for their form M24-7(1-86) or an updated one. This will explain the abbreviations for championship titles, obedience titles, and other valuable information by which you may make an intelligent evaluation from the pedigree of the puppy or adult purebred dog in which you have an interest.

Show and/or obedience titles do not indicate the highest degree of physical beauty or trainability, field trial titles indicate performance to a greater degree, but do not necessarily indicate a conformation to the breed standard. In deciding which puppy you want, based on what you want for your puppy, now is the time when knowledge of your English Springer Spaniel puppy's parents' bloodlines and performance of their ancestors of the past three generations will be of value. They will tell you for sure what the line is capable of.

If you are properly prepared for your search for the English Springer Spaniel you want, you will make a decision you will not regret, but which will lead you and your family to a better, fuller and happier life with a Springer Spaniel.

Choose a puppy that is alert and active, with bright eyes and a shining coat.

CARING for Your English Springer Spaniel

When you bought your Springer puppy, the seller should have filled you in on what the puppy was being fed. Keep the puppy on this food for at least the first few weeks to avoid digestive problems. Diarrhea is especially serious in young puppies because it can cause them to dehydrate very rapidly. Such rapid dehydration can lead to severe problems—even death.

Not only should you feed the same kind of food as the breeder/seller, you should stick to the same schedule of feedings. For an eight- to ten-week-old puppy, this will be four small meals a day. Your puppy will be your best guide regarding how much to feed while he's growing quickly. You do not want to overfeed him, because that can be stressful on his developing bones; on the other hand, you certainly don't want to underfeed him. You should be able to tell if you're going too far in either direction, because overly-fat Springer puppies look too roly-poly and underfed Springers' ribs will protrude. In either extreme, the pup's energy will be off, too. Again, follow the seller's advice, and if you have any doubts or questions, call him or her.

By the time your Springer pup is six months old—and for the rest of his life—he can be fed just two meals a day. Two meals are better than one for many reasons. Like us, dogs enjoy their mealtimes, and for that reason, two is better than one. Two meals lessens the amount of food eaten at one time, which is better for the digestive system. A Springer may be less inclined

to gulp at his food if he's getting it twice a day

Puppies receive their first nourishment from their mother, but by the time they are ready to be sold they should be eating nutritionally balanced dog food.

Reputable breeders start their puppies on the road to good nutrition, so stick with your pup's original diet when you first bring him home, making any changes gradually.

instead of once, thereby lessening the chance of getting a gassy stomach or worse, bloat.

To keep your Springer from becoming a fussy eater, prepare the food, put it down for the dog and leave it down no longer than 15 minutes. Unless your dog's a really slow eater, that is plenty of time to finish one meal. If he only eats some of the meal and walks away, pick up the bowl and dispose of the remaining food. Don't feel sorry for him and substitute his unfinished dog food with table scraps or other people food, and don't start doctoring his dinner with more "goodies" than dog food or your dog will soon have you trained to feed him only what he wants—which could get expensive and will be bad for his overall health. If your dog just isn't eating, take him to the veterinarian immediately for a check up.

If you want to change your English Springer Spaniel puppy's diet for any reason, it should be done gradually, over a period of several meals and a few days. Begin by adding a tablespoon or two of the new food, gradually increasing the amount until the meal consists entirely of the new product.

About Dog Food

In order for a canine diet to qualify as "complete and balanced" in the United States, it must must meet standards set by the American Association of Feed Control Officials (AAFCO). These standards ensure that the food has adequate amounts of nutrients such as proteins, carbohydrates, vitamins and minerals. Manufacturers are required to list the product ingredients on the label. They are in descending order, with the most prevalent ingredient listed first.

A complete and nutritionally balanced diet will be evident in your English Springer Spaniel's shiny coat and overall healthy appearance.

Dog foods come in three forms: dry (kibble), wet (canned) and semi-moist. Most owners feed approximately 75% kibble and 25% canned. The canned food has the most flavor and smell, which dogs love; the kibble is the better choice economically and nutritionally, because you get more for your money, and the hard pieces help fight plaque and tartar formation.

Canine nutrition is its own field of study and millions are spent developing dog foods. A quality commercial food and plenty of cool, fresh water will provide your dog with the essential nutrients in correct proportions.

Your Springer will let you know if the food you give him is doing its job. Assuming he's getting the exercise and grooming he needs, are his eyes clear and bright? Is his coat lustrous and shiny, free of scaly, bald or inflammed spots? Does his weight look and feel good; that is, can you feel his ribs under a layer of supple skin? Is his energy level right, neither too hyper nor too passive (discuss your Springer's energy level with his breeder if it seems out of proportion in either extreme). If your Springer looks and feels the picture of good health, then your food is doing its job.

Raising your dog's food and water dishes and giving him two meals a day will reduce his tendency to gulp down his food and lessen his chances of bloat.

The owners of dogs with special dietary needs now have a number of commercially prepared diets to choose from. There are foods for overweight, underweight or geriatric dog as well as puppies and growing dogs. There are foods for dogs with food allergies and other medical problems. Before switching to any of these special foods, consult with your veterinarian. He or she will best be able to advise you regarding the needs of your individual dog.

ALL-IMPORTANT EXERCISE

If you want to know what kind of exercise would be best for your Springer, just think about what he was bred to do: hunt all day. Spaniels are in heaven when they can hunt large fields, and will enthusiastically snuffle through every hedgerow they come across looking for birds.

Springers are not high-energy dogs, but they do enjoy daily exercise and the chance to go outdoors where they can utilize their natural instincts.

Unfortunately, most owners don't live in areas that have large fields in which they can leisurely walk with their dogs off-leash. Large parks are good substitutes, and your Springer will love you for getting him to one

near you. Be absolutely sure your dog will come to you when called before turning him loose in a large, open area. He can disappear in no time and be lost to you forever.

Though Springers will gladly accompany you in the fields all day, they are not high-energy dogs, and will do fine with a few brisk walks a day (and that special romp in the park once a week). They can be trained to trot alongside you while you're jogging or bicycling, will play fetch in the yard, and will relish playtime with you.

Springers are hardy athletes and will tolerate cold and heat so long as they're in shape and you don't push them. Have plenty of cool water on hand in warm weather and try to work in the cooler mornings and evenings; in wintertime, give a working dog more food for fuel and warmth, and make sure he's completely dried off and has a warm comfy bed to curl up in at night.

It's important to exercise your Springer's body *and* mind.

Springers are highly trainable and intelligent dogs, and love to participate in organized sports like tracking, agility and hunting.

He was bred to work well with people and is highly trainable. Besides basic obedience, teach him games like "find it," "speak," "sit up," and others you can create yourself or learn from a book. Both of you will have a fun mind-and-body workout doing this together. Organized sports like obedience, agility, tracking and, of course, hunting, are all things your well-trained English Springer Spaniel will love. Check them out!

GROOMING YOUR SPRINGER

With his fine-textured, flat or wavy, medium-length coat, the Springer needs regular grooming to keep mats from forming or burrs from getting tangled in the fine hair. The feathering on the Springer's chest, legs and belly is especially susceptible to getting tangled this way.

You're lucky you have a dog who needs regular grooming, because it is an excellent way to catch health problems before they become catastrophes. It is also a relaxing time for you and your dog. Regular grooming promotes healthy skin and coat by removing dead skin, cleaning the hairs and stimulating the hair follicles.

You will need some special equipment to groom your Springer. This includes a pin brush, a soft-bristle brush, a regular and a fine-toothed comb, a pair of sharp scissors, electric clippers and a nail clipper and/or grinder.

How often you brush your Springer will depend on how thick and long his coat is. Also, shedding dogs need daily brushing to remove the dead hairs. Don't let more than a couple of days go by between grooming sessions to keep your Springer looking and feeling his best.

When you groom your Springer, start by brushing him all over. It helps to work with a grooming "table," one you can put your dog on so you don't have to bend over the whole time.

Following a regular grooming regimen is an excellent way to detect any health or coat problems, as well as a great way to spend relaxing quality time with your dog.

Start grooming your English Springer Spaniel by letting him stand or lie down on a non-skid table and brush his coat with a soft-bristle brush.

Buy an existing table or put a piece of non-skid matting on a table. Your dog will learn to stand or lay down on it.

After brushing, go over your dog with the fine-toothed comb. Explore any bumps or scratches you encounter and treat them with ointment if necessary.

Remove any discharge from around your Springer's eyes with a damp cloth or cotton ball. Check your Springer's ears. They should be pink and dry inside. Because the Springer has long, droopy ears, this ear care is very important. It is easy for bacteria to grow and spread in the warm, dark environment of the Springer's inner ear. Use a commercial ear-cleaning formula to gently swab out any dirt you see in the ear. Don't work too forcefully—you don't want to push dirt further in the ear or puncture the ear canal. If you notice a cheesy smell, your Springer may have an infection for which your veterinarian may need to prescribe medication. Call and check with your vet.

Next, examine his feet. Don't let his nails get too long. If you can hear them clicking on the floor, they're too long. To clip your dog's nails, take the paw in your hand and, with clippers specially made for dogs, snip just the end off. You don't want to sever the quick, or vein running through the nail. This will bleed and hurt the dog. Train your dog to accept nail clipping by starting slow and gentle. Don't let your dog get the upper hand, however. Some protesting on his part is normal. As long as you're not hurting him, he should be taught to endure this not-always-pleasant experience. Praise him profusely for being good and he'll eventually be unfazed by the clipping. If the whole thing proves too much of a hassle and

When you bathe your Springer Spaniel, make sure to rinse his coat thoroughly. Excess shampoo can cause skin irritation.

chore for you, ask your veterinarian or a professional groomer to do the job for you.

A well-groomed Springer should only need a bath every few weeks or months, depending on how dirty he becomes. To bathe your Springer, soak his coat thoroughly with warm water, shampoo his entire body (avoiding his face), then rinse thoroughly. And I mean thoroughly. Unrinsed shampoo can irritate the skin. Towel-dry your dog and run the wet towel over his face to buff-clean it. If you want, you can blow-dry your dog; keep the setting down, though, or you might burn his skin. If it's warm enough outside, you can let your dog air-dry—but keep an eye on him because he may run to the nearest mudhole to reannoint himself with the scent he finds most appealing!

If you are interested in showing your Springer, you will need to study the grooming techniques of experienced handlers, including the correct ways to scissor and trim the coat. Grooming for the show ring is an art that takes years to master.

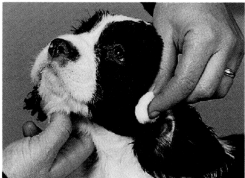

Your Springer's long ears will need to be kept clean to prevent the growth of bacteria. Check your dog's ears regularly and gently remove any dirt with a cotton swab.

TRAINING the English Springer Spaniel

I could count into the hundreds the number of people I have assisted to train their dogs. Training a dog is not an easy task, but it can be accomplished when you understand where you are going and the progressive steps that need to be taken to get there. You need to learn the teaching skills that will be required, and acquire knowledge on the subject that you will be teaching. You must then figure out how to apply this knowledge and skill to produce the finished product: a well-trained dog. If you have properly prepared yourself and your family for this training, you are well on your way to having a great deal of future satisfaction with this addition to your family.

Basic obedience training is necessary for your puppy, not only to teach him acceptable behavior, but to keep him safe as well.

First of all, you must establish who your pupil is. If it is a puppy, then you must start a pre-school training plan. A good rule of thumb to remember in regard to the age of the puppy is that one month in the age of your dog is equal to one year in the age of a child. This will guide you through the puppy's first twelve months. You do not,

or should not, scold or punish in any way a puppy under five months of age. No matter how they behave, they are only doing what a canine of that age is supposed to do. Your job is to know how to train and guide them using positive associations between acts and cues.

You must get your own act together before you can teach the dog a command with an associated cue and decide exactly what it is that you want the puppy or adult dog to do. No matter what papers his sire and dam possess, your untrained puppy or older dog does not know what will be required of

Crates make housetraining your pet much easier, because dogs do not want to soil where they eat and sleep.

him or what he is supposed to do when you give a command. Your words are just a lot of human noise to him, so be clear. Start with a list of the cues and acts you are going to teach as a basic training foundation. We will assume you have selected your puppy one or two weeks after it has been weaned, usually at about eight weeks of age.

CRATE TRAINING AND HOUSEBREAKING

If you are keeping the dog in the house, select a place that can be all his own. A crate with a soft blanket on the bottom makes a cozy den for your dog. Crates are also excellent aids to housebreaking, because puppies and dogs do not want to eliminate where they sleep. Crates also help keep puppies on schedule. Buy a crate that your puppy will be comfortable in as an adult. Until he's full grown, divide it so the pup fits comfortably in one-half of the crate. Make the crate appealing by lining it with an old, soft towel or blanket. Incorporate leaving the pup in his crate into his schedule for feeding, playing, etc. Place the crate near an accessible area to be used for potty training. This may be on multiple pieces of paper, lain over a water proof undersheet to prevent seepage to the floor area in case of accidents, or near a door. Through this door, take the puppy into the yard every couple of hours, or shortly after he eats, drinks water, wakes up, plays vigorously or if he seems to fidget a little more than usual. Take him outside and walk quickly to the area where you want him to relieve himself. Do this in a gentle and business-like manner, using a cue to indicate an association with the act the puppy is about to perform. Praise him when he is finished and he will quickly pick up what is expected of him.

If you acquire an older puppy, you will have to take a different approach to establish yourself as the leader of the pack. By five months of age, you are dealing with an animal that is close to a five-year-old child in maturity. Your puppy's education can be accelerated a little with the use of a slip-chain collar and some additional force; as firm as necessary, as gentle as possible. Use clear cues, proper responses, praise and encouragement when earned, and scolding when needed. Always stop after each cue and proper response and end the session with praise. Remember to keep your lesson short. A few minutes of training can sometimes be more productive than a half-hour of mixed responses coupled with a scolding or a display of anger on your part.

I am neither extremely patient nor do I always control my temper. But I have learned through experience that if I do not control myself, I am going to reverse the things I have already taught and make it necessary to expend more time to correct the mistake I made.

LEARNING CUES

To begin, use your dog's name before each command or cue you practice, such as sit, stay, down, come, get in the car, or fetch. This is for two primary reasons. First, it will get the dog's attention, and secondly it will let the dog know that the cue applies to him. For instance, at some later time you may have two dogs in a kennel or dog crate, or may send one of a group of Springers to perform a retrieve. By using the dog's name and accustoming him to respond to it, you can maintain control of one or more dogs, designating which dog is to act.

Most writers and trainers use the cue "no." I try not to use this command. It is purely negative and I like to accentuate the positive in training. I prefer "leave it," or another learned cue, such as sit, come, "hie," kennel or whatever it will take stop the dog from performing the unwanted behavior. To me, "no" is similar to "stay." If I give a dog the cue, "stay," that indicates that the dog should stop whatever he is doing and wait until he's given another cue.

The "come" command is one of the most important lessons your dog will learn to ensure his safety and well-being. Jennifer Sweet and Metro practice recall exercises.

A big step toward training an eager retriever is to teach the "Dog's Name-Come!" command.

This English Springer Spaniel practices the "down" command with his owner Gail Jackson.

This is one of the most important exercises you will ever teach your Springer. He should always associate coming to you with a pleasant experience, so he will come willingly. You should never scold or punish your dog after giving him the "come" command. To teach his retrieving skills, you should toss a training retrieve dummy, a knotted sock, or an old glove out on the lawn and at the same time say, "Dog's Name-Fetch!" The sole purpose is to have the puppy or newly started dog race to the object, pick it up, race back to you, and deliver it gently to your hand. At this time, after you have your hands firmly on the retrieved object, attempt to gently remove the object from the puppy's mouth. If a bit of a tug-o-war takes place, try to distract the puppy and slip the object from its mouth as you say, "Give!" If it looks like the puppy or dog will make another retrieve, repeat the lesson.

If you are able to get another retrieve, stop. I do no more than three retrieves in one training session.

When you prepare your puppy's food, cue him to come to the location where you will feed him. At this time, teach the puppy, "Hup!" (Hup is an old English term, commonly used in the United States by Springer Spaniel handlers in place of sit.) This act and cue are easily taught to the young dog or adult dog at feeding time. Before placing a food dish in front of the dog, command, "Hup" and if necessary, place the dog in the sitting position as you start to put the food down. Do not make the puppy or dog remain for any extended time at the food bowl, no longer than a second or two, then give the release cue. Follow all correct responses with praise to let the dog know you are pleased with the performance. To stop a Springer Spaniel out in a bird field at a considerable distance, possibly as much as one hundred yards or more give one blast of a whistle: that is "Hup" until another visual or whistle cue is given. The verbal cue (hup) and a visual cue, such as an upraised arm or hand, used together are examples of advanced training and must be taught and enforced until a firmly established response is obtained.

Puppy obedience classes will not only help both you and your Springer master proper training exercises, they will also allow your puppy time to socialize with other dogs.

Do your best to develop empathy, establish rapport, earn the dog's respect, and give the dog your respect. Do not tease a puppy or dog of any age. Do not rough-house with the puppy or allow him to sink his little sharp teeth into you, then punish him. Playful puppies will nip and bite each other, not drawing blood or causing great pain. They have not learned that human skin is different from theirs. When a puppy nips you, cry as if you were injured. When any dog learns he has hurt you in play, he will become gentler.

It is also important to enroll your puppy in obedience classes as soon as possible. I recommend obedience class in order to help not only your Springer, but to give you the proper training and guidance you need to be a good teacher. If you have access to a professional sporting dog trainer and you are interested in using your Springer Spaniel as a hunting dog, you should make an appointment with the trainer.

Another option is to associate with an amateur, but experienced, trainer who has the qualifications to give you proper guidance. However, be careful when selecting your trainer because it might turn out to be a case of the blind leading the blind, and you will end up learning bad training practices as well as good ones. Also, do not take your new dog or puppy to a trap or skeet range or introduce it suddenly to gunshot. In every case that I am aware of, gun shyness has been the result of poor or improper introductory training. An introduction to the hunting fields does not require that game be shot or guns be discharged. It is enough to let your Springer enjoy walking through the fields or woodlands where he can become familiar with the different types of life that exist there. Remember, however, that it is necessary to be in an area that is safe for both you and your dog. Some areas may have uncovered holes, bogs or other dangers, such as nearby roads. If your Springer becomes excited and starts to chase a bird or rabbit, he might come to harm. Even if you do not plan to be a hunter, or train for or participate in field trials, you should complete a personal course in the obedience requirements of any responsible dog owner.

Every experience, whether good or bad, affects your dog's attitude towards training. If he has positive experiences in the field, your Springer will be eager to hunt with you.

Obviously, every experience, good or bad, physical or psychological, genetic or environmental, affects the personality of any animal and must be dealt with as the trainer approaches the task of training. These experiences can make the job of keeping, training, feeding and living with a dog either easy or difficult. That is where the challenge lies, and when you are properly prepared, any problems that may exist can be overcome and excellent results obtained and maintained. I have heard people say, "It must take a lot of patience to train a dog." Actually, it does not take much patience if it is something you like and know how to do. When you understand the need for training, and appreciate the value of a well-trained dog, it becomes a challenge to prepare yourself to do the best possible job you can.

Your Springer's crate should be made into a cozy den where he can relax. Line it with a soft blanket and provide him with toys to make him feel right at home

If you wish to eventually hunt with your Springer Spaniel puppy, slowly introduce him to the field in a safe area. Nick Campanelli takes his puppy on his first field outing.

FIELD TRAINING

Training the English Springer Spaniel or any other dog for hunting or field trials requires the knowledge and understanding of the techniques of training. Having had experience with a considerable number of breeds of sporting dogs, I feel comfortable in saying that a well-bred Springer Spaniel has a greater desire to please than do the other sporting dog breeds. One of the places they are in their real element is in the hunting field, working birds or rabbits, upland or water fowl in all kinds of weather, in all kinds of vegetation. As an all-purpose gun-dog, as well as a family pet, they are an easy dog for anyone to train and handle if the owner has the interest in preparing for the task.

The English Springer Spaniel's natural love for the outdoors and great desire to please make him an instinctual and enthusiastic hunting breed.

Early in his training, your new puppy or older dog should be introduced to the hunting fields and the animals that reside there. An introduction to the field is good exercise for both you and your Springer Spaniel, and the smells and creatures he will encounter will bring out the innate hunting characteristics of his wild canine ancestors who once hunted for their food.

TRAINING AIDS

A training aid can be considered a variety of persons, places or things that will assist you in training your dog for hunting. When I first began training, bird shots or BB gun shots, either from a .22 caliber weapon or from a Y-shaped sling-shot, were often used to control a dog that was at a distance from the trainer in a field. I have found after several years of dog training that it is possible to train a dog without the use of bird shot or other propelled objects.

Today the electronic transmitter receiver combination is often used to stimulate the dog to properly respond to a cue. I have watched many handlers use the electronic collar, and have taken part in field trials and hunt tests with people who

Leads enable you to give your Springers enough leeway to sniff about but still keep them under your control.

have used it. I have never seen results by professional or amateur trainers that have convinced me that they are necessary to obtain a proper result from a well-bred sporting dog. They can help a professional sporting dog trainer who has a large number of dogs to train. Many trainers are not that well qualified and one often sees unsound dogs being used in a hunting field, still wearing an electronic collar.

Great working and sporting dogs were being trained a long time before these "training aids" were available, and I know a sound dog can be trained without them, if the course of training is properly approached. I have successfully trained a number of top working gun dogs without using any of these projectiles or electronic collars. I have trained a top field trial champion, a high-point puppy, and a Master Hunter who was the high-point puppy on the West coast and second in the U.S., all without the use of projectiles or electronic collars.

There are other training aids that are helpful, such as tables used to teach the dog to retrieve, to hold a point, or to respond to the cues to sit, hup, or whoa. It saves the trainer's back if he has a large number of dogs he is working with each day.

Leads

Other training aids include three types of leads, one of the most useful is what I call a "field lead." It is made from a leather strap of one-inch to one- and one-quarter-inch in width, about the thickness of the rein of a horse bridle, and *Training dummies* about 48 inches long. It is made by *will be very helpful in* folding the strap in such a way as to *assisting you train* make a loop of about six inches to use *your English Springer* as a handle, and allowing about six *Spaniel for hunting* inches for a loop on the bottom end *and retrieving.* to use for a swivel snap. A slip-chain training collar is then attached on the snap. Use the proper weight and size collar for dogs of different sizes. Use the lightest slip-chain collar possible to handle the weight of the dog.

Another lead, one I call my "long line," is half of a 50-foot section of window sash cord, commonly sold in hardware stores. To this I attach a slip-chain training collar using a bowline knot, a common knot which is easy to tie and to untie, in spite of the amount of tension placed on it. I also tie a similar knot at the other end to use as a grip or handle when controlling the dog in training. It is wise to wear gloves if you have tender hands; in any case, never try to stop a dog if the line is running through your hands, or it will burn them severely.

51

A third type of lead is a six-foot leather or nylon line commonly used by obedience ring trainers. This is good for walking your dog, and enables you to give him enough leeway to sniff about, but still keep him under close control.

Whistles

Another handling aid I recommend is a plastic field whistle. Dogs respond better at a distance to whistle signals than they do to voices, which can become garbled on a windy day or a high, dry cover. The most commonly used whistle signals for a sporting dog are one sharp blast to signal "Hup," two sharp blasts to signal "pay attention," and sharply repeated trills to signal "come in." This last whistle signal should be taught, enforced, and re-enforced, because "come" is one of the most important commands a dog can know. The whistle can be heard for a greater distance than a voice and will often bring a lost or missing dog back if it is within hearing distance.

Canvas or plastic training dummies, sometimes called bumpers, make a very useful addition to your training aids, not only for the several ways they can be used, but for the excellent exercise the long retrieves of up to two or three hundred yards can provide. They can also be used to teach "fetch," which should be prefaced by the dog's name.

FIELD TRAINING

At the start of training, command the dog to get in the sitting position and roll a small plastic or canvas covered

With the proper field training, your English Springer Spaniel will move on from dummies to game in no time.

retrieving dummy into the dog's mouth by pressing in, down and back. As you roll the dummy into the dog's mouth, cue "fetch." You want to teach the cue "fetch" to the dog that has shown it has the option to go from where he is to where the object to be retrieved lies when told "(Name) - Fetch." This is it: the dog's name, followed by fetch (meaning, go from where you are to the object, and return it as soon as possible), then hold the object until after I have placed my hands on it and have given the release command or cue. I use "give." "Give" tells the dog to let the object be taken gently from his mouth. "Fetch" is thus the cue for the entire act of retrieving. There is no point in adding words such as hold it, take, etc. It is helpful to use praise or the already learned cue "come" to encourage the dog to perform the act of retrieving properly. When any part of the retrieving act is

Teach your Springer to "fetch" by rolling a plastic retrieving dummy in his mouth, throwing it and having him bring it back to your hand on your cue.

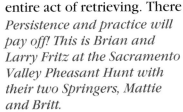

Persistence and practice will pay off! This is Brian and Larry Fritz at the Sacramento Valley Pheasant Hunt with their two Springers, Mattie and Britt.

performed in a proper manner, even for a few seconds, praise and encouragement is warranted. At this point, with proper encouragement and praise, you will be half-way to mastering what is required of a properly trained sporting dog. The next step is to have the dog carry the object to your hand and release on the cue "give."

Remember, the final objective is to have your dog race to retrieve the object, race back to place it in your hands, and on the cue "give," release it gently into your hand. We are not concerned with having the dog sit and wait to be sent or to sit before giving the object up. This might tend to cramp the retrieving style of your dog if practiced too early in his training.

When the dog is thoroughly proficient in the basic act of retrieving, you can teach him some new rules to this game. The dog will retrieve without permission or cue the air borne object, which in and of itself means hup, sit or whoa.

This can be taught in your yard with a dummy and a short field lead. As you walk with the dog at heel on

Early in training, the objective is to get the dog to retrieve and return the dummy. Always remember to praise him generously when he obeys.

Accustoming your Springer Spaniel to the scents of the game and the field will make him more receptive to training exercises.

your left, toss the dummy out into the yard with your right hand. Allow the object to travel a few feet in the air, so that the dog can track its movement. Keep the dog from running after the dummy by pulling him up with the lead and slip-chain training collar. Do not give a verbal or visual command, including foot or body movement which might indicate a cue to sit or hup. The purpose of this lesson is to teach the dog that when he sees anything fly into the air, he should stop or sit until given a further cue. As soon as the object has hit the ground, release the snap or drop the lead and send the dog to make the retrieve. The retrieve should be made as previously taught.

Praise your dog generously when he responds properly. Repeat the exercise three times. It is preferable that this lesson is separated from other lessons by an hour or more. As with all lessons, three sets of short periods is much better than a few or too many lessons of long duration.

Retrieving in water is usually no trouble for the Springer Spaniel and until a few years back, I was of the opinion that spaniels loved the water and that water retrieves were natural to them. But Tee Dude, one of my first English Springer Spaniels, had almost convinced me otherwise, although he did become acclimated after a while. It is best to introduce the dogs to water when they are young, with their dam or littermates. If this does not succeed, and they do not take to the water on their own or with some encouragement, you may have to wade out into shallow, but swimming depth, water and call the puppy or dog to you. When he has reached swimming depth, walk a little farther out, and then walk to the shore. Repeat this, wading a little deeper and walking a little farther each time until the dog gains confidence. Then you can try a short retrieve into swimming depth water. It should be no problem from there. The first introduction to water should not be during the cold months in

If your Springer seems wary of water, acclimate him to it slowly by wading in with him, gradually leading him to deeper areas.

icy water, although most dogs, particularly a well-bred English Springer Spaniel, have no problem with reasonable exposure to icy water and sub-zero air temperatures. English Springer Spaniels, if properly bred, are a hardy breed, and I have hunted from a goose blind with a Springer at four degrees below zero. However, they do need more food and some extra fat when used for hunting, particularly in low temperatures.

Once field training skills are taught and learned, they become a part of your dog's life, just as other properly taught cues and commands will be. Persistence, ingenuity and practice will get the job done within a reasonable amount of time, the result being a product of your ability as a trainer and the ability of your pupil.

Although most Springers love the water, an early and cautious introduction to water retrieval will avoid any fearful reactions.

SPORT of Purebred Dogs

Welcome to the exciting and sometimes frustrating sport of dogs. No doubt you are trying to learn more about dogs or you wouldn't be deep into this book. This section covers the basics that may entice you, further your knowledge and help you to understand the dog world. If you decide to give showing, obedience or any other dog activities a try, then I suggest you seek further help from the appropriate source.

Dog showing has been a very popular sport for a long time and has been taken quite seriously by some. Others only enjoy it as a hobby.

The Kennel Club in England was formed in 1859, the American Kennel Club was established in 1884 and the Canadian Kennel Club was formed in 1888. The purpose of these clubs was to register purebred dogs and maintain their Stud Books. In the beginning, the concept of registering dogs was not readily accepted. More than 36 million dogs have been enrolled in the AKC Stud Book since its inception in 1888. Presently the kennel clubs not only register dogs but adopt and enforce rules and regulations governing dog shows, obedience trials and field trials. Over the years they have fostered and encouraged interest in the health and welfare of the purebred dog. They routinely donate funds to veterinary research for study on genetic disorders.

Following are the addresses of the kennel clubs in the United States, Great Britain and Canada.

With persistence, patience and praise, your versatile English Springer Spaniel puppy will become a well-trained and obedient companion.

The American Kennel Club
51 Madison Avenue
New York, NY 10010
(Their registry is located at:
5580 Centerview Drive, STE 200
Raleigh, NC 27606-3390)

The Kennel Club
1 Clarges Street
Piccadilly, London, WIY 8AB
England

The Canadian Kennel Club
111 Eglinton Avenue
East Toronto, Ontario M6S 4V7
Canada

Today there are numerous activities that are enjoyable for both the dog and the handler. Some of the activities include conformation showing, obedience competition, tracking, agility, the Canine Good Citizen Certificate, and a wide range of instinct tests that vary from breed to breed. Where you start depends upon your goals which early on may not be readily apparent.

PUPPY KINDERGARTEN

Every puppy will benefit from this class. PKT is the foundation for all future dog activities from conformation to "couch potatoes." Pet owners should make an effort to attend even if they never expect to show their dog. The class is

All Springer puppies can benefit from early training to teach them basic obedience and good manners.

designed for puppies about three months of age with graduation at approximately five months of age. All the puppies will be in the same age group and, even though some may be a little unruly, there should not be any real problem. This class will teach the puppy some beginning obedience. As in all obedience classes the owner learns how to train his own dog. The PKT class gives the puppy the opportunity to interact with other puppies in the same age group and exposes him to strangers, which is very important. Some dogs grow up

Use your dog's name when giving him a command and be sure to establish good eye contact. Metro performs the "down" on the command of his owner Jennifer Sweet.

with behavior problems, one of them being fear of strangers. As you can see, there can be much to gain from this class.

There are some basic obedience exercises that every dog should learn. Some of these can be started with puppy kindergarten.

Sit

One way of teaching the sit is to have your dog on your left side with the leash in your right hand, close to the collar. Pull up on the leash and at the same time reach around his hindlegs with your left hand and tuck them in. As you are doing this say, "Beau, sit." Always use the dog's name when you give an active command. Some owners like to use a treat holding it over the dog's head. The dog will need to sit to get the treat. Encourage the dog to hold the sit for a few seconds, which will eventually be the beginning of the Sit/Stay. Depending on how cooperative he is, you can rub him under the chin or stroke his back. It is a good time to establish eye contact.

Down

Sit the dog on your left side and kneel down beside

There are basic commands that every dog should know how to perform. Art Perle's Springers Tee Dude and Sunny demonstrate the "sit."

him with the leash in your right hand. Reach over him with your left hand and grasp his left foreleg. With your right hand, take his right foreleg and pull his legs forward while you say, "Beau, down." If he tries to get up, lean on his shoulder to encourage him to stay down. It will relax your dog if you stroke his back while he is down. Try to encourage him to stay down for a few seconds as preparation for the Down/Stay.

Heel

The definition of heeling is the dog walking under control at your left heel. Your puppy will learn controlled walking in the puppy kindergarten class, which will eventually lead to heeling. The command is "Beau, heel," and you start off briskly with your left foot. Your leash is in your right hand and your left hand is holding it about half way down. Your left hand should be able to control the leash and there should be a little slack in it. You want him to walk with you with

In conformation, your dog is judged on how closely he conforms to the standard of the breed.

your leg somewhere between his nose and his shoulder. You need to encourage him to stay with you, not forging (in front of you) or lagging behind you. It is best to keep him on a fairly short lead. Do not allow the lead to become tight. It is far better to give him a little jerk when necessary and remind him to heel. When you come to a halt, be prepared physically to make him sit. It takes practice to become coordinated. There are excellent books on training that you may wish to purchase. Your instructor should be able to recommend one for you.

Recall

This quite possibly is the most important exercise you will ever teach. It should be a pleasant experience. The puppy may learn to do random recalls while being attached to a long line such as a clothes line. Later the exercise will start with the dog sitting and staying until called. The command is "Beau, come."

"Heel" is another important basic command. Your Springer should learn to walk at your side at a controlled and steady pace.

Let your command be happy. You want your dog to come willingly and faithfully. The recall could save his life if he sneaks out the door. In practicing the recall, let him jump on you or touch you before you reach for him. If he is shy, then kneel down to his level. Reaching for the insecure dog could frighten him, and he may not be willing to come again in the future. Lots of praise and a treat would be in order whenever you do a recall. Under no circumstances should you ever correct your dog when he has come to you. Later in formal obedience your dog will be required to sit in front of you after recalling and then go to heel position.

CONFORMATION

Conformation showing is our oldest dog show sport. This type of showing is based on the dog's appearance–that is his structure, movement and attitude. When considering this type of showing, you need to be aware of your breed's standard and be able to evaluate your dog compared to that standard. The breeder of your puppy or other experienced breeders would be good sources for such an evaluation. Puppies can go through lots of changes over a period of time. I always say most puppies start out as promising hopefuls and then after maturing may be disappointing as show candidates. Even so this should not deter them from being excellent pets.

Usually conformation training classes are offered by the local kennel or obedience clubs. These are excellent places for training puppies. The puppy should be able to walk on a lead before entering such a class. Proper ring procedure and technique for posing (stacking) the dog will be demonstrated as well as gaiting the dog. Usually certain patterns are used in the ring such as the triangle or the "L." Conformation class, like the PKT class, will give your youngster the opportunity to socialize with different breeds of dogs and humans too.

It takes some time to learn the routine of conformation showing. Usually one starts at the puppy matches which may be AKC Sanctioned or Fun Matches. These matches are generally for puppies from two or three months to a year old, and there may be classes for the adult over the age of 12 months. Similar to point shows, the classes are divided by sex and after completion of the classes in that breed or variety, the class winners compete for Best of Breed or Variety. The winner goes on to compete in the Group and the Group winners compete for Best in Match. No championship points are awarded for match wins.

A few matches can be great training for puppies even though there is no intention to go on showing. Matches enable the puppy to meet new people and be handled by a stranger— the judge. It is also a change of environment, which broadens the horizon for both dog and handler. Matches and other dog

activities boost the confidence of the handler and especially the younger handlers.

Sandy Furuicawa grooms her show prospect to get him looking his best for the ring.

Your dog must get used to being in the show ring and being handled by judges if he is to compete in conformation.

Earning an AKC championship is built on a point system, which is different from Great Britain. To become an AKC Champion of Record the dog must earn 15 points. The number of points earned each time depends upon the number of dogs in competition. The number of points available at each show depends upon the breed, its sex and the location of the show. The United States is divided into ten AKC zones. Each zone has its own set of points. The purpose of the zones is to try to equalize the points available from breed to breed and area to area. The AKC adjusts the point scale annually.

The number of points that can be won at a show are between one and five. Three-, four- and five-point wins are considered majors. Not only does the dog need 15 points won under three different judges, but those points must include two majors under two different judges. Canada also works on a point system but majors are not required.

Dogs always show before bitches. The classes available to those seeking points are: Puppy (which may be divided into 6 to 9 months and 9 to 12 months); 12 to 18 months; Novice; Bred-by-Exhibitor; American-bred; and Open. The class winners of the same sex of each breed or variety compete against each other for Winners Dog and Winners Bitch. A Reserve Winners Dog and Reserve Winners Bitch are also awarded but do not carry any points unless the Winners win is disallowed by AKC. The Winners Dog and Bitch compete with the specials (those dogs that have attained championship) for Best of Breed or Variety, Best of Winners and Best of Opposite Sex. It is possible to pick up an extra point or even a major if the points are higher for the defeated winner than those of Best of Winners. The latter would get the higher total from the defeated winner.

At an all-breed show, each Best of Breed or Variety winner will go on to his respective Group and then the Group winners will compete against each other for Best in Show. There are seven Groups: Sporting, Hounds, Working, Terriers, Toys, Non-Sporting and Herding. Obviously there are no Groups at speciality shows (those shows that have only one breed or a show such as the American Spaniel Club's Flushing Spaniel Show, which is for all flushing spaniel breeds).

Earning a championship in England is somewhat different since they do not have a point system. Challenge Certificates are awarded if the judge feels the dog is deserving regardless of the number of dogs in competition. A dog must earn three Challenge Certificates under three different judges, with at least one of these Certificates being won after the age of 12 months. Competition is very strong and entries may be higher than they are in the U.S. The Kennel Club's Challenge Certificates are only available at Championship Shows.

In England, The Kennel Club regulations require that certain dogs, Border Collies and Gundog breeds, qualify in a working capacity (i.e., obedience or field trials) before becoming a full Champion. If they do not qualify in the working aspect, then they are designated a Show Champion, which is equivalent to the AKC's Champion of Record. A Gundog may be granted the title of Field Trial Champion (FT Ch.) if it passes all the tests in the field but would also have to qualify in conformation before becoming a full Champion. A Border Collie that earns the title of Obedience Champion (Ob Ch.) must also qualify in the conformation ring before becoming a Champion.

The U.S. doesn't have a designation full Champion but does award for Dual and Triple Champions. The Dual Champion must be a Champion of Record, and either Champion Tracker, Herding Champion, Obedience Trial Champion or Field Champion. Any dog that has been awarded the titles of Champion of Record, and any two of the following: Champion Tracker, Herding Champion, Obedience Trial Champion or Field Champion, may be designated as a Triple Champion.

The shows in England seem to put more emphasis on breeder judges than those in the U.S. There is much competition within the breeds. Therefore the quality of the individual breeds should be very good. In the United States we tend to have more "all around judges" (those that judge multiple breeds) and use the breeder judges at the specialty shows. Breeder judges are more familiar with their own breed since they are actively breeding that breed or did so at one time. Americans emphasize Group and Best in Show wins and promote them accordingly.

Handlers must pose their show dogs in the most flattering position to emphasize the dog's specific strengths and hide any flaws.

It is my understanding that the shows in England can be very large and extend over several days, with the Groups being scheduled on different days. I believe there is only one all-breed show in the U.S. that extends over two days, the Westminster Kennel Club Show. In our country we have cluster shows, where several different clubs will use the same show site over consecutive days.

Westminster Kennel Club is our most prestigious show although the entry is limited to 2500. In recent years, entry has been limited to Champions. This show is more formal than the majority of the shows with the judges wearing formal attire and the handlers fashionably dressed. In most instances the quality of the dogs is superb. After all, it is a show of

Champions. It is a good show to study the AKC registered breeds and is by far the most exciting—especially since it is televised! WKC is one of the few shows in this country that is still benched. This means the dog must be in his benched area during the show hours except when he is being groomed, in the ring, or being exercised.

Typically, the handlers are very particular about their appearances. They are careful not to wear something that will detract from their dog but will perhaps enhance it. American ring procedure is quite formal compared to that of other countries. I remember being reprimanded by a judge because I made a suggestion to a friend holding my second dog outside the ring. I certainly could have used more discretion so I would not call attention to myself. There is a certain etiquette expected between the judge and exhibitor and among the other exhibitors. Of course it is not always the case but the judge is supposed to

Successful showing requires dedication and preparation, but most of all, it should be an enjoyable experience for handlers and dogs alike.

be polite, not engaging in small talk or even acknowledging that he knows the handler. I understand that there is a more informal and relaxed atmosphere at the shows in other countries. For instance, the dress code is more casual. I can see where this might be more fun for the exhibitor and especially for the novice. This country is very handler-oriented in many of the breeds. It is true, in most instances, that the experienced professional handler can present the dog better and will have a feel for what a judge likes.

In England, Crufts is The Kennel Club's own show and is most assuredly the largest dog show in the world. They've been known to have an entry of nearly 20,000, and the show lasts four days. Entry is only gained by qualifying through winning in specified classes at another Championship Show. Westminster is strictly conformation, but Crufts exhibitors and spectators enjoy not only conformation but obedience, agility and a multitude of exhibitions as well. Obedience was admitted in 1957 and agility in 1983.

Handlers must wear comfortable, practical clothing that does not distract attention from the dog they are showing.

If you are handling your own dog, please give some consideration to your apparel. For sure the dress code at matches is more informal than the point shows. However, you should wear something a little more appropriate than beach attire or ragged jeans and bare feet. If you check out the handlers and see what is presently fashionable, you'll catch on. Men usually dress with a shirt and tie and a nice sports coat. Whether you are male or female, you will want to wear comfortable clothes and shoes. You need to be able to run with your dog and you certainly don't want to take a chance of falling and hurting yourself. Heaven forbid, if nothing else, you'll upset your dog. Women usually wear a dress or two-piece outfit, preferably with pockets to carry bait, comb, brush, etc. In this case men are the lucky ones with all their pockets. Ladies, think about where your dress will be if you need to kneel on the floor and also think about running. Does it allow freedom to do so?

Junior handling is a wonderful way for a young person to build confidence and a strong foundation for successful future showing and handling.

Years ago, after toting around all the baby paraphernalia, I found toting the dog and necessities a breeze. You need to take along dog; crate; ex pen (if you use one); extra newspaper; water pail and water; all required grooming equipment, including hair dryer and extension cord; table; chair for you; bait for dog and lunch for you and friends; and, last but not least, clean up materials, such as plastic bags, paper towels, and perhaps a bath towel and some shampoo—just in case. Don't forget your entry confirmation and directions to the show.

If you are showing in obedience, then you will want to wear pants. Many of our top obedience handlers wear pants that are color-coordinated with their dogs. The philosophy is that imperfections in the black dog will be less obvious next to your black pants.

Whether you are showing in conformation, Junior Showmanship or obedience, you need to watch the clock and be sure you are not late. It is customary to pick up your conformation armband a few minutes before the start of the class. They will not wait for you and if you are on the show grounds and not in the ring, you will upset everyone. It's a little more complicated picking up your obedience armband if you show later in the class. If you have not picked up your armband and they get to your number, you may not be allowed to show. It's best to pick up your armband early, but then you may show earlier than expected if other handlers don't pick up. Customarily all conflicts should be discussed with the judge prior to the start of the class.

Handlers must gait their dogs around the ring so the judges can evaluate their movement and body conformation.

Junior Showmanship

The Junior Showmanship Class is a wonderful way to build self confidence even if there are no aspirations of

staying with the dog-show game later in life. Frequently, Junior Showmanship becomes the background of those who become successful exhibitors/ handlers in the future. In some instances it is taken very seriously, and success is measured in terms of wins. The Junior Handler is judged solely on his ability and skill in presenting his dog. The dog's conformation is not to be considered by the judge. Even so the condition and grooming of the dog may be a reflection upon the handler.

Usually the matches and point shows include different classes. The Junior Handler's dog may be entered in a breed or obedience class and even shown by another person in that class. Junior Showmanship classes are usually divided by age and perhaps sex. The age is determined by the handler's age on the day of the show. The classes are:

Novice Junior for those at least ten and under 14 years of age who at time of entry closing have not won three first places in a Novice Class at a licensed or member show.

Novice Senior for those at least 14 and under 18 years of age who at the time of entry closing have not won three first places in a Novice Class at a licensed or member show.

Open Junior for those at least ten and under 14 years of age who at the time of entry closing have won at least three first places in a Novice Junior Showmanship Class at a licensed or member show with competition present.

Open Senior for those at least 14 and under 18 years of age who at time of entry closing have won at least three first places in a Novice Junior Showmanship Class at a licensed or member show with competition present.

Junior Handlers must include their AKC Junior Handler number on each show entry. This needs to be obtained from the AKC.

CANINE GOOD CITIZEN

The AKC sponsors a program to encourage dog owners to train their dogs. Local clubs perform the pass/fail tests, and dogs who pass are awarded a Canine Good Citizen Certificate. Proof of vaccination is required at the time of participation. The test includes:

1. Accepting a friendly stranger.
2. Sitting politely for petting.
3. Appearance and grooming.
4. Walking on a loose leash.
5. Walking through a crowd.
6. Sit and down on command/staying in place.

Excelling in obedience competition is easy for working dogs like the Springer Spaniel that are used to following orders from their masters.

7. Come when called.
8. Reaction to another dog.
9. Reactions to distractions.
10. Supervised separation.

If more effort was made by pet owners to accomplish these exercises, fewer dogs would be cast off to the humane shelter.

OBEDIENCE

Obedience is necessary, without a doubt, but it can also become a wonderful hobby or even an obsession. In my opinion, obedience classes and competition can provide wonderful companionship, not only with your dog but with your classmates or

Canine Good Citizens must be able to get along with all kinds of people, including children. This Springer looks like he has passed the test.

fellow competitors. It is always gratifying to discuss your dog's problems with others who have had similar experiences. The AKC acknowledged Obedience around 1936, and it has changed tremendously even though many of the exercises are basically the same. Today, obedience competition is just that—very competitive. Even so, it is possible for every obedience exhibitor to come home a winner (by earning qualifying scores) even though he/she may not earn a placement in the class.

Most of the obedience titles are awarded after earning three qualifying scores (legs) in the appropriate class under three different judges. These classes offer a perfect score of 200, which is extremely rare. Each of the class exercises has its own point value. A leg is earned after receiving a score of at least 170 and at least 50 percent of the points available in each exercise. The titles are:

Companion Dog—CD

This is called the Novice Class and the exercises are:

1. Heel on leash and figure 8	40 points
2. Stand for examination	30 points
3. Heel free	40 points
4. Recall	30 points

5. Long sit—one minute   30 points
6. Long down—three minutes   30 points
Maximum total score   200 points

Companion Dog Excellent—CDX

This is the Open Class and the exercises are:

1. Heel off leash and figure 8   40 points
2. Drop on recall   30 points
3. Retrieve on flat   20 points
4. Retrieve over high jump   30 points
5. Broad jump   20 points
6. Long sit—three minutes (out of sight)   30 points
7. Long down—five minutes (out of sight)   30 points
Maximum total score   200 points

Utility Dog—UD

The Utility Class exercises are:

1. Signal Exercise   40 points
2. Scent discrimination-Article 1   30 points
3. Scent discrimination-Article 2   30 points
4. Directed retrieve   30 points
5. Moving stand and examination   30 points
6. Directed jumping   40 points
Maximum total score   200 points

After achieving the UD title, you may feel inclined to go after the UDX and/or OTCh. The UDX (Utility Dog Excellent) title went into effect in January 1994. It is not easily attained. The title requires qualifying simultaneously ten times in Open B and Utility B but not necessarily at consecutive shows.

The OTCh (Obedience Trial Champion) is awarded after the dog has earned his UD and then goes on to earn 100 championship points, a first place in Utility, a first place in Open and another first place in either class. The placements must be won under three different judges at all-breed obedience trials. The points are determined by the number of dogs competing in the Open B and Utility B classes. The OTCh title precedes the dog's name.

Obedience matches (AKC Sanctioned, Fun, and Show and Go) are usually available. Usually they are sponsored by the local obedience clubs. When preparing an obedience dog for a title, you will find matches very helpful. Fun Matches and Show and Go Matches are more lenient in allowing you to make corrections in the ring. I frequently train (correct) in the ring and inform the judge that I would like to do so and to please mark me "exhibition." This means that I will not be eligible for any prize. This type of training is usually very necessary for the Open and Utility Classes. AKC Sanctioned Obedience Matches do not allow corrections in the ring since they must abide by the AKC Obedience Regulations. If you are interested in showing in obedience, then you should contact the AKC for a copy of the Obedience Regulations.

Training for any type of competition or activity allows the owner and his dog develop a closeness through working together.

TRACKING

Tracking is officially classified obedience, but I feel it should have its own category. There are three tracking titles available: Tracking Dog

(TD), Tracking Dog Excellent (TDX), Variable Surface Tracking (VST). If all three tracking titles are obtained, then the dog officially becomes a CT (Champion Tracker). The CT will go in front of the dog's name.

A TD may be earned anytime and does not have to follow the other obedience titles. There are many exhibitors that prefer tracking to obedience, and there are others like myself that do both. In my experience with small dogs, I prefer to earn the CD and CDX before attempting tracking. My reasoning is that small dogs are closer to the mat in the obedience rings and therefore it's too easy to put the nose down and sniff. Tracking encourages

Tracking tests are used to evaluate a dog's natural abilities. Hunting dogs like the Springer instinctively use their noses.

sniffing. Of course this depends on the dog. I've had some dogs that tracked around the ring and others (TDXs) who wouldn't think of sniffing in the ring.

Tracking Dog–TD

A dog must be certified by an AKC tracking judge that he is ready to perform in an AKC test. The AKC can provide the names of tracking judges in your area that you can contact for certification. Depending on where you live, you may have to travel a distance if there is no local tracking judge. The certification track will be equivalent to a regular AKC track. A regulation track must be 440 to 500 yards long with at least two right-angle turns out in the open. The track will be aged 30 minutes to two hours. The handler has two starting flags at the beginning of the track to indicate the direction started. The dog works on a harness and 40-foot lead and must work at least 20 feet in front of the handler. An article (either a dark glove or wallet) will be dropped at the end of the track, and the dog must indicate it but not necessarily retrieve it.

People always ask me what the dog tracks. In my opinion, initially, the beginner on the short-aged track tracks the

Because of their extensive background in field work, the English Springer Spaniel does very well in tracking competitions.

tracklayer. Eventually the dog learns to track the disturbed vegetation and learns to differentiate between tracks. Getting started with tracking requires reading the AKC regulations and a good book on tracking plus finding other tracking enthusiasts. I like to work on the buddy system. That is—we lay tracks for each other so we can practice blind tracks. It is possible to train on your own, but if you are a beginner, it is a lot more entertaining to track with a buddy. Tracking is my favorite dog sport. It's rewarding seeing the dog use his natural ability.

Tracking Dog Excellent—TDX

The TDX track is 800 to 1000 yards long and is aged three to five hours. There will be five to seven turns. An article is left at the starting flag, and three other articles must be indicated on the track. There is only one flag at the start, so it is a blind start. Approximately one and a half hours after the track is laid, two tracklayers will cross over the track at two different places to test the dog's ability to stay with the original track. There will be at least two obstacles on the track such as a change of cover, fences, creeks, ditches, etc. The dog must have a TD before entering a TDX. There is no certification required for a TDX.

Variable Surface Tracking—VST

This test came into effect September 1995. The dog must have a TD earned at least six months prior to entering this test. The track is 600 to 800 yards long and shall have a minimum of three different surfaces. Vegetation shall be included along with two areas devoid of vegetation such as concrete, asphalt, gravel, sand, hard pan

Agility competition is growing in popularity. This English Springer Spaniel tries the teeter-totter.

A Springer clears the bar jump in agility. Agility is definitely a spectator sport!

or mulch. The areas devoid of vegetation shall comprise at least one-third to one-half of the track. The track is aged three to five hours. There will be four to eight turns and four numbered articles including one leather, one plastic, one metal and one fabric dropped on the track. There is one starting flag. The handler will work at least 10 feet from the dog.

AGILITY

Agility was first introduced by John Varley in England at the Crufts Dog Show, February 1978, but Peter Meanwell, competitor and judge, actually developed the idea. It was officially recognized in the early '80s. Agility is extremely popular in England and Canada and growing in popularity in the U.S. The AKC acknowledged agility in August 1994. Dogs must be at least 12 months of age to be entered. It is a fascinating sport that the dog, handler and spectators enjoy to the utmost. Agility is a spectator sport! The dog performs off lead. The handler either runs with his dog or positions himself on the course and directs his dog with verbal and hand signals

over a timed course over or through a variety of obstacles including a time out or pause. One of the main drawbacks to agility is finding a place to train. The obstacles take up a lot of space and it is very time consuming to put up and take down courses.

The titles earned at AKC agility trials are Novice Agility Dog (NAD), Open Agility Dog (OAD), Agility Dog Excellent (ADX), and Master Agility Excellent (MAX). In order to acquire an agility title, a dog must earn a qualifying score in its respective class on three separate occasions under two different judges. The MAX will be awarded after earning ten qualifying scores in the Agility Excellent Class.

PERFORMANCE TESTS

During the last decade the American Kennel Club has promoted performance tests—those events that test the different breeds' natural abilities. This type of event encourages a handler to devote even more time to his dog and retain the natural instincts of his breed heritage. It is an important part of the wonderful world of dogs.

Agility is just one of the many activities in which Springer Spaniels can demonstrate their athletic and competitive prowess.

Lure Coursing

For all sighthounds (Afghans, Basenjis, Borzois, Greyhounds, Ibizans, Irish Wolfhounds, Pharaoh Hounds, Rhodesian Ridgebacks, Salukis, Scottish Deerhounds, and Whippets).

The participant must be at least one year of age, and dogs with limited registration (ILP) are elgible. They chase a lure of three plastic bags and are judged on overall ability, follow, speed, agility and endurance. Like the other AKC performance tests, lure coursing gives dogs the opportunity to prove themselves at what they were originally bred to do.

Agility tests like the tire jump allow the Springer to apply his natural abilities to the competition ring.

Junior Courser (JC) A hound running alone shall receive certification from a judge on one date, and a second certification at a later time, stating the hound completed a 600-yard course with a minimum of four turns. The hound must complete the course with enthusiasm and without interruption.

Senior Courser (SC) Must be eligible to enter the open stake and the hound must run with at least one other hound. Must receive qualifying scores at four AKC-licensed or member trials under two different judges.

Field Championship (FC) Prefix to the hound's name. Must receive 15 championship points including two first placements with three points or more under two different judges.

Earthdog Events

For small terriers (Australian, Bedlington, Border, Cairn, Dandie Dinmont, Fox (Smooth & Wire), Lakeland, Norfolk, Norwich, Scottish, Sealyham, Skye, Welsh, West Highland White and Dachshunds).

Limited registration (ILP) dogs are eligible and all entrants must be at least six months of age. The primary purpose of the small terriers and Dachshunds is to pursue quarry to ground, hold the game, and alert the hunter where to dig, or to bolt. There are two parts to the test: (1) the approach to the quarry and (2) working the quarry. The dog must pass both parts for a Junior Earthdog (JE). The Senior Earthdog (SE) must do a third part—to leave the den on command. The Master Earthdog (ME) is a bit more complicated.

Hunting Titles

For retrievers, pointing breeds and spaniels. Titles offered are Junior Hunter (JH), Senior Hunter (SH), and Master Hunter (MH).

Flushing Spaniels Their primary purpose is to hunt, find,

The primary purpose of flushing spaniels such as the Springer is to hunt, find, flush and return birds quickly to hand as pleasantly as possible.

flush and return birds to hand as quickly as possible in a pleasing and obedient manner. The entrant must be at least six months of age and dogs with limited registration (ILP) are eligible. Game used are pigeons, pheasants, and quail.

Retrievers Limited registration (ILP) retrievers are not eligible to compete in Hunting Tests. The purpose of a Hunting Test for retrievers is to test the merits of and evaluate the abilities of retrievers in the field in order

Retrieving skills are inherent in Springer Spaniels, which is why they are used in field trials and hunting competition.

Hunting tests measure a Springer's skill in the field to determine if he is a suitable and competent hunting companion.

to determine their suitability and ability as hunting companions. They are expected to retrieve any type of game bird, pheasants, ducks, pigeons, guinea hens and quail.

Pointing Breeds Are eligible at six months of age, and dogs with limited registration (ILP) are permitted. They must show a keen desire to hunt; be bold and independent; have a fast, yet attractive, manner of hunting; and demonstrate intelligence not only in seeking objectives but also in the ability to find game. They must establish point, and in the more advanced tests they need to be steady to wing and must remain in position until the bird is shot or they are released.

A Senior Hunter must retrieve. A Master Hunter must honor. The judges and the marshal are permitted to ride horseback during the test, but all handling must be done on foot.

Your English Springer Spaniel must be able to find and retrieve all kinds of game, including pigeons, pheasant and quail.

Herding Titles

For all Herding breeds and Rottweilers and Samoyeds.

Entrants must be at least nine months of age and dogs with limited registration (ILP) are eligible. The Herding program is divided into Testing and Trial sections. The goal is to demonstrate proficiency in herding livestock in diverse situations. The titles offered are Herding Started

(HS), Herding Intermediate (HI), and Herding Excellent (HX). Upon completion of the HX a Herding Championship may be earned after accumulating 15 championship points.

The above information has been taken from the AKC Guidelines for the appropriate events.

Schutzhund

The German word "Schutzhund" translated to English means "Protection Dog." It is a fast growing competitive sport in the United States and has been popular in England since the early 1900s. Schutzhund was originally a test to determine which German Shepherds were quality dogs for breeding in Germany.

Nick Campanelli, a judge of trials and hunting tests and a field trainer since 1965, comes out of the field after a successful demonstration of work and handling.

It gives us the ability to test our dogs for correct temperament and working ability. Like every other dog sport, it requires teamwork between the handler and the dog.

Schutzhund training and showing involves three phases: Tracking, Obedience and Protection. There are three SchH levels: SchH I (novice), SchH II (intermediate), and SchH III (advanced). Each title becomes progressively more difficult. The handler and dog start out in each phase with 100 points. Points are deducted as errors are incurred. A total perfect score is 300, and for a dog and handler to earn a title he must earn at least 70 points in tracking and obedience and at least 80 points in protection. Today many different breeds participate successfully in Schutzhund.

GENERAL INFORMATION

Obedience, tracking and agility allow the purebred dog with an Indefinite Listing Privilege (ILP) number or a limited registration to be exhibited and earn titles. Application must be made to the AKC for an ILP number.

The American Kennel Club publishes a monthly *Events* magazine that is part of the *Gazette*, their official journal for the sport of purebred dogs. The *Events* section lists upcoming shows and the secretary or superintendent for them. The majority of the conformation shows in the U.S. are overseen by licensed superintendents. Generally the entry closing date is approximately two-and-a-half weeks before the actual show. Point shows are fairly expensive, while the match shows cost about one third of the point show entry fee. Match shows usually take entries the day of the show but some are pre-entry. The best way to find match show information is through your local kennel club. Upon asking, the AKC can provide you with a list of superintendents, and you can write and ask to be put on their mailing lists.

Showing your Springer takes time, dedication and teamwork, but you and your dog can only benefit from the bond that will form between you.

Obedience trial and tracking test information is available through the AKC. Frequently these events are not superintended, but put on by the host club. Therefore you would make the entry with the event's secretary.

As you have read, there are numerous activities you can share with your dog. Regardless what you do, it does take teamwork. Your dog can only benefit from your attention and training. I hope this chapter has enlightened you and hope, if nothing else, you will attend a show here and there. Perhaps you will start with a puppy kindergarten class, and who knows where it may lead!

There are so many activities that you and your puppy can participate in and the versatile Springer has the ability to excel at them all!

TRAVELING with Your Dog

The earlier you start traveling with your new puppy or dog, the better. He needs to become accustomed to traveling. However, some dogs are nervous riders and become carsick easily. It is helpful if he starts with an empty stomach. Do not despair, as it will go better if you continue taking him with you on short fun rides. How would you feel if every time you rode in the car you stopped at the doctor's for an injection? You would soon dread that nasty car. Older dogs that tend to get carsick may have more of a problem adjusting to traveling. Those dogs that are having a serious problem may benefit from some medication prescribed by the veterinarian.

The earlier you take your Springers traveling with you, the quicker they will become accustomed to riding in a car.

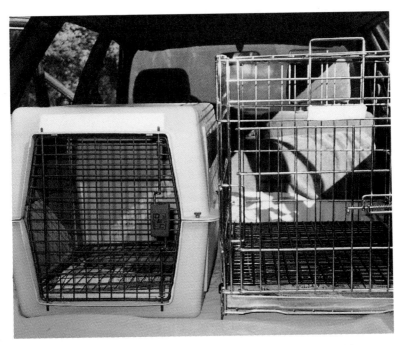

Crates are a safe way for your dog to travel. The fiberglass crates are safest, but the metal crates allow for more air.

Do give your dog a chance to relieve himself before getting into the car. It is a good idea to be prepared for a clean up with a leash, paper towels, bag and terry cloth towel.

The safest place for your dog is in a fiberglass crate, although close confinement can promote carsickness in some dogs. If your dog is nervous you can try letting him ride on the seat next to you or in someone's lap.

An alternative to the crate would be to use a car harness made for dogs and/or a safety strap attached to the harness or collar. Whatever you do, do not let your dog ride in the back of a pickup truck unless he is securely tied on a very short lead. I've seen trucks stop quickly and, even though the dog was tied, it fell out and was dragged.

I do occasionally let my dogs ride loose with me because I really enjoy their companionship, but in all honesty they are safer in their crates. I have a friend whose van rolled in an accident but his dogs, in their fiberglass crates, were not injured nor did they escape. Another advantage of the crate is that it is a safe place to leave him if you need to run into the store. Otherwise you wouldn't be able to leave the windows down. Keep in mind that while many dogs are overly protective in their crates, this may not be enough to deter dognappers. In some states it is against the law to leave a dog in the car unattended.

Never leave a dog loose in the car wearing a collar and leash. I have known more than one dog that has killed himself by hanging. Do not let him put his head out an open window. Foreign debris can be blown into his eyes. When leaving your dog unattended in a car, consider the temperature. It can take less than five minutes to reach temperatures over 100 degrees Fahrenheit.

TRIPS

Perhaps you are taking a trip. Give consideration to what is best for your dog–traveling with you or boarding. When traveling by car, van or motor home, you need to think ahead about locking your vehicle. In all probability you have many valuables in the car and do not wish to leave it unlocked. Perhaps most valuable and not replaceable is your dog. Give thought to securing your vehicle and providing adequate ventilation for him. Another consideration for you when traveling with your dog is medical problems that may arise and little inconveniences, such as exposure to external parasites. Some areas of the country are quite flea infested. You may want to carry flea spray with you. This is even a good idea when staying in motels. Quite possibly you are not the only occupant of the room.

Unbelievably many motels and even hotels do allow canine guests, even some very first-class ones. Gaines Pet Foods

Corporation publishes *Touring With Towser*, a directory of domestic hotels

Be careful that you do not let your dog hang his head out of the window while you are driving. Debris might fly into his eyes and ears or he may be injured.

If you accustom your dog to traveling when they are puppies, they will be eager to follow you wherever you go!

and motels that accommodate guests with dogs. Their address is Gaines TWT, PO Box 5700, Kankakee, IL, 60902. I would recommend you call ahead to any motel that you may be considering and see if they accept pets. Sometimes it is necessary to pay a deposit against room damage. Of course you are more likely to gain accommodations for a small dog than a large dog. Also the management feels reassured when you mention that your dog will be crated. Since my dogs tend to bark when I leave the room, I leave the TV on nearly full blast to deaden the noises outside that tend to encourage my dogs to bark. If you do travel with your dog, take along plenty of baggies so that you can clean up after him. When we all do our share in cleaning up, we make it possible for motels to continue accepting our pets. As a matter of fact, you should practice cleaning up everywhere you take your dog.

Depending on where your are traveling, you may need an up-to-date health certificate issued by your veterinarian. It is good policy to take along your dog's medical information, which would include the name, address and phone number of your veterinarian, vaccination record, rabies certificate, and any medication he is taking.

AIR TRAVEL

When traveling by air, you need to contact the airlines to check their policy. Usually you have to make arrangements up to a couple of weeks in advance for traveling with your dog.

You may consider boarding your dog in a kennel if you go away.

The airlines require your dog to travel in an airline approved fiberglass crate. Usually these can be purchased through the airlines but they are also readily available in most pet-supply stores. If

your dog is not accustomed to a crate, then it is a good idea to get him acclimated to it before your trip. The day of the actual trip you should withhold water about one hour ahead of departure and no food for about 12 hours. The airlines generally have temperature restrictions, which do not allow pets to travel if it is either too cold or too hot. Frequently these restrictions are based on the temperatures at the departure and arrival airports. It's best to inquire about a health certificate. These usually need to be issued within ten days of departure. You should arrange for non-stop, direct flights and if a commuter plane should be involved, check to see if it will carry dogs. Some don't. The Humane Society of the United States has put together a tip sheet for airline traveling. You can receive a copy by sending a self-addressed stamped envelope to:

The Humane Society of the United States
Tip Sheet
2100 L Street NW
Washington, DC 20037.

Regulations differ for traveling outside of the country and are sometimes changed without notice. Well in advance you

If you decide to bring your Springer with you when you travel, bring along some familiar things, like his toys and his crate, to make him feel at home.

need to write or call the appropriate consulate or agricultural department for instructions. Some countries have lengthy quarantines (six months), and countries differ in their rabies vaccination requirements. For instance, it may have to be given at least 30 days ahead of your departure.

Do make sure your dog is wearing proper identification. You never know when you might be in an accident and separated from your dog. Or your dog could be frightened and somehow manage to escape and run away. When I travel, my dogs wear collars with engraved nameplates with my name, phone number and city.

Another suggestion would be to carry in-case-of-emergency instructions. These would include the address and phone number of a relative or friend, your veterinarian's name, address and phone number, and your dog's medical information.

BOARDING KENNELS

Because they are such accommodating dogs, English Springer Spaniels usually get used to traveling quickly and enjoy visiting different places.

Perhaps you have decided that you need to board your dog. Your veterinarian can recommend a good boarding facility or possibly a pet sitter that will come to your house. It is customary for the boarding kennel to ask for proof of vaccination for the DHLPP, rabies and bordetella vaccine. The bordetella should have been given within six months of boarding. This is for your protection. If they do not ask for this proof I would not board at their kennel. Ask about flea control. Those dogs that suffer flea-bite allergy can get in trouble at a boarding kennel. Unfortunately boarding kennels are limited on how much they are able to do.

For more information on pet sitting, contact NAPPS:
National Association of Professional Pet Sitters
1200 G Street, NW
Suite 760
Washington, DC 20005.

Our clinic has technicians that pet sit and technicians that board clinic patients in their homes. This may be an alternative for you. Ask your veterinarian if they have an employee that can help you. There is a definite advantage of having a technician care for your dog, especially if your dog is on medication or is a senior citizen.

You can write for a copy of *Traveling With Your Pet* from ASPCA, Education Department, 441 E. 92nd Street, New York, NY 10128.

Most airlines and hotels have policies concerning traveling with pets, so be sure to check it out thoroughly before making plans.

IDENTIFICATION and Finding the Lost Dog

There are several ways of identifying your dog. The old standby is a collar with dog license, rabies, and ID tags. Unfortunately collars have a way of being separated from the dog and tags fall off. I am not suggesting you shouldn't use a collar and tags. If they stay intact and on the dog, they are the quickest way of identification.

For several years owners have been tattooing their dogs. Some tattoos use a number with a registry. Here lies the problem because there are several registries to check. If you wish to tattoo, use your social security number. The humane shelters have the means to trace it. It is usually done on the inside of the rear thigh. The area is first shaved and numbed. There is no pain, although a few dogs do not like the buzzing sound. Occasionally tattooing is not legible and needs to be redone.

The newest method of identification is microchipping. The microchip is a computer chip that is no larger than a grain of rice. The veterinarian implants it by injection between the shoulder blades. The dog feels no discomfort. If your dog is lost and picked up by the humane society, they can trace you by scanning the microchip, which has its own code. Microchip scanners are friendly to other brands of microchips and their registries. The microchip comes with a dog tag saying the dog

Your Springer will be curious about his environment and other dogs when you take him out. Always keep him on a lead to prevent him from wandering off without you.

is microchipped. It is the safest way of identifying your dog.

Finding The Lost Dog

I am sure you will agree with me that there would be little worse than losing your dog. Responsible pet owners rarely lose their dogs. They do not let their dogs run free because they don't want harm to come to them. Not only that but in most, if not all, states there is a leash law.

Make sure your dog wears a collar with tags at all times. This will increase your chances of being reunited should become separated.

Beware of fenced-in yards. They can be a hazard. Dogs find ways to escape either over or under the fence. Another fast exit is through the gate that perhaps the neighbor's child left unlocked.

The newest method of identification is microchipping. The microchip is no bigger than a grain of rice.

Below is a list that hopefully will be of help to you if you need it. Remember don't give up, keep looking. Your dog is worth your efforts.

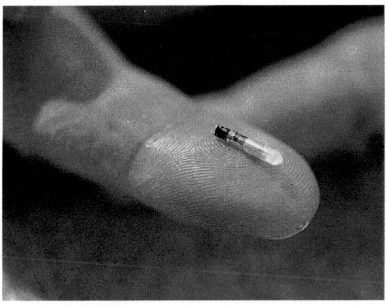

1. Contact your neighbors and put flyers with a photo on it in their mailboxes. Information you should include would be the dog's name, breed, sex, color, age, source of identification, when your dog was last seen and where, and your name and phone numbers. It may be helpful to say the dog needs medical care. Offer a *reward*.

2. Check all local shelters daily. It is also possible for your dog to be picked up away from home and end up in an out-of-the-way shelter. Check these too. Go in person. It is not good enough to call. Most shelters are limited on the time they can hold dogs then they are put up for adoption or euthanized. There is the possibility that your dog will not make it to the shelter for several days. Your dog could have been wandering or someone may have tried to keep him.

Make sure you have a clear, recent picture of your dog to distribute in case he becomes lost.

3. Notify all local veterinarians. Call and send flyers.

4. Call your breeder. Frequently breeders are contacted when one of their breed is found.

5. Contact the rescue group for your breed.

6. Contact local schools—children may have seen your dog.

7. Post flyers at the schools, groceries, gas stations, convenience stores, veterinary clinics, groomers and any other place that will allow them.

8. Advertise in the newspaper.

9. Advertise on the radio.

Make sure your doors are securely closed to keep your puppy from escaping or getting injured.

HEALTH CARE

Veterinary medicine has become far more sophisticated than what was available to our ancestors. This can be attributed to the increase in household pets and consequently the demand for better care for them. Also human medicine has become far more complex. Today diagnostic testing in veterinary medicine parallels human diagnostics. Because of better technology we can expect our pets to live healthier lives thereby increasing their life spans.

Puppies are very vulnerable when they are first born. They should see the veterinarian for a check-up within 48 to 72 hours of their birth.

THE FIRST CHECK UP

You will want to take your new puppy/ dog in for its first check up within 48 to 72 hours after acquiring it. Many breeders

By breeding only the best quality dogs, good health and temperament is passed down to each new generation. strongly recommend this check up and so do the humane shelters. A puppy/dog can appear healthy but it may have a serious problem that is not apparent to the layman. Most pets have some type of a minor flaw that may never cause a real problem.

Unfortunately if he/she should have a serious problem, you will want to consider the consequences of keeping the pet and the attachments that will be formed, which may be broken prematurely. Keep in mind there are many healthy dogs looking for good homes.

This first check up is a good time to establish yourself with the veterinarian and learn the office policy regarding their hours and how they handle emergencies. Usually the breeder or another conscientious pet owner is a good reference for locating a capable veterinarian. You should be aware that not all veterinarians give the same quality of service. Please do not make your selection on the least expensive clinic, as they may be short changing your pet. There is the possibility that eventually it will cost you more due to improper diagnosis, treatment, etc. If you are selecting a new veterinarian, feel free to ask for a tour of the clinic. You should inquire about making an appointment for a tour since all clinics are working clinics, and therefore may not be available all day for sightseers. You may worry less if you see where your pet will be spending the day if he ever needs to be hospitalized.

THE PHYSICAL EXAM

Your veterinarian will check your pet's overall condition, which includes listening to the heart; checking the respiration; feeling the abdomen, muscles and joints; checking the mouth, which includes the gum color and signs of gum disease along with plaque buildup; checking the ears for signs of an infection or ear mites; examining the eyes; and, last but not least, checking the condition of the skin and coat.

A change in your Springer's behavior may indicate a health problem. See your veterinarian immediately if you suspect something is wrong.

He should ask you questions regarding your pet's eating and elimination habits and invite you to relay your questions. It is a good idea to prepare a list so as not to forget anything. He should discuss the proper diet and the quantity to be fed. If this should differ from your breeder's recommendation, then you should convey to him the breeder's choice and see if he approves. If he recommends changing the diet, then this should be done over a few days so as not to cause a gastrointestinal upset. It is customary to take in a fresh stool sample (just a small amount) for a test for intestinal parasites. It must be fresh, preferably within 12 hours, since the eggs hatch quickly and after hatching will not be observed under the microscope. If your pet isn't obliging then, usually the technician can take one in the clinic.

IMMUNIZATIONS

It is important that you take your puppy/dog's vaccination record with you on your first visit. In case of a puppy,

Find out which vaccinations your puppy has received prior to your bringing him home, for his health as well as the health of your family.

presumably the breeder has seen to the vaccinations up to the time you acquired custody. Veterinarians differ in their vaccination protocol. It is not unusual for your puppy to have received vaccinations for distemper, hepatitis, leptospirosis, parvovirus and parainfluenza every two to three weeks from the age of five or six weeks. Usually this is a combined injection and is typically called the DHLPP. The DHLPP is given through at least 12 to 14 weeks of age, and it is customary to continue with another parvovirus vaccine at 16 to 18 weeks. You may wonder why so many immunizations are necessary. No one knows for sure when the puppy's maternal antibodies are gone, although it is customarily accepted that distemper antibodies are gone by 12 weeks. Usually parvovirus antibodies are gone by 16 to 18 weeks of age. However, it is possible for the maternal antibodies to be gone at a much earlier age or even a later age. Therefore immunizations are started at an early age. The vaccine will not give immunity as long as there are maternal antibodies.

The rabies vaccination is given at three or six months of age depending on your local laws. A vaccine for bordetella (kennel cough) is advisable and can be given anytime from the age of five weeks. The coronavirus is not commonly given unless there is a problem locally. The Lyme vaccine is necessary in endemic areas. Lyme disease has been reported in 47 states.

Distemper

This is virtually an incurable disease. If the dog recovers, he is subject to severe nervous disorders. The virus attacks every tissue in the body and resembles a bad cold with a fever. It can cause a runny nose and eyes and cause gastrointestinal disorders, including a poor appetite, vomiting and diarrhea. The virus is carried by raccoons, foxes, wolves, mink and other dogs. Unvaccinated youngsters and senior citizens are very susceptible. This is still a common disease.

Hepatitis

This is a virus that is most serious in very young dogs. It is spread by contact with an infected animal or its stool or urine. The virus affects the liver and kidneys and is characterized by high fever, depression and lack of appetite. Recovered animals may be afflicted with chronic illnesses.

Dogs that live in close quarters can transmit diseases to one another easily if not properly vaccinated. Be sure to keep your Springer's immunization record up-to-date.

Leptospirosis

This is a bacterial disease transmitted by contact with the urine of an infected dog, rat or other wildlife. It produces severe symptoms of fever, depression, jaundice and internal bleeding and was fatal before the vaccine was developed. Recovered dogs can be carriers, and the disease can be transmitted from dogs to humans.

The deer tick is the most common carrier of Lyme disease. Photo courtesy of Virbac Laboratories, Inc., Fort Worth, Texas.

Parvovirus

This was first noted in the late 1970s and is still a fatal disease. However, with proper vaccinations, early diagnosis and prompt treatment, it is a manageable disease. It attacks the bone marrow and intestinal tract. The symptoms include depression, loss of appetite, vomiting, diarrhea and collapse. Immediate medical attention is of the essence.

Rabies

This is shed in the saliva and is carried by raccoons, skunks, foxes, other dogs and cats. It attacks nerve tissue, resulting in paralysis and death. Rabies can be transmitted to people and is virtually always fatal. This disease is reappearing in the suburbs.

Bordetella (Kennel Cough)

The symptoms are coughing, sneezing, hacking and retching accompanied by nasal discharge usually lasting from a few days to several weeks. There are several disease-producing organisms responsible for this disease. The present vaccines are helpful but do not protect for all the strains. It usually is not life threatening but in some instances it can progress to a serious bronchopneumonia. The disease is highly contagious. The vaccination should be given routinely for dogs that come in contact with other dogs, such as through boarding, training class or visits to the groomer.

Coronavirus

This is usually self limiting and not life threatening. It was first noted in the late '70s about a year before parvovirus. The virus produces a yellow/brown stool and there may be depression, vomiting and diarrhea.

Lyme Disease

This was first diagnosed in the United States in 1976 in Lyme, CT in people who lived in close proximity to the deer tick. Symptoms may include acute lameness, fever, swelling of joints and loss of appetite. Your veterinarian can advise you if you live in an endemic area.

After your puppy has completed his puppy vaccinations, you will continue to booster the DHLPP once a year. It is customary to booster the rabies one year after the first vaccine and then, depending on where you live, it

Hookworms are almost microscopic intestinal worms that can cause anemia and therefore serious problems, and even death.

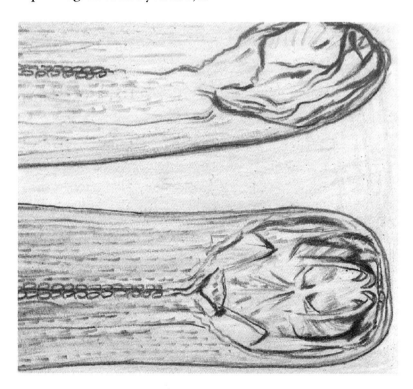

should be boostered every year or every three years. This depends on your local laws. The Lyme and corona vaccines are boostered annually and it is recommended that the bordetella be boostered every six to eight months.

ANNUAL VISIT

I would like to impress the importance of the annual check up, which would include the booster vaccinations, check for intestinal parasites and test for heartworm. Today in our very busy world it is rush, rush and see "how much you can get for how little." Unbelievably, some non-veterinary businesses have entered into the vaccination business. More harm than good can come to your dog through improper vaccinations, possibly from inferior vaccines and/or the wrong schedule. More than likely you truly care about your companion dog and over the years you have devoted much time and expense to his well being. Perhaps you are unaware that a vaccination is not just a vaccination. There is more involved. Please, please follow through with regular physical examinations. It is so important for your veterinarian to know your dog and this is especially true during middle age through the geriatric years. More than likely your older dog will require more than one physical a year. The annual physical is good preventive medicine. Through early diagnosis and subsequent treatment your dog can maintain a longer and better quality of life.

Check your Springer Spaniel's coat carefully after he has been playing outside for any external parasites like fleas or ticks.

INTESTINAL PARASITES

Hookworms

These are almost microscopic intestinal worms that can cause anemia and therefore serious problems, including death, in young puppies. Hookworms can be transmitted to humans through penetration of the skin. Puppies may be born with them.

Roundworms

These are spaghetti-like worms that can cause a potbellied appearance and dull coat along with more severe symptoms, such as vomiting, diarrhea and coughing. Puppies acquire these while in the mother's uterus and through lactation. Both hookworms and roundworms may be acquired through ingestion.

Whipworms

These have a three-month life cycle and are not acquired through the dam. They cause intermittent diarrhea usually with mucus. Whipworms are possibly the most difficult worm to eradicate. Their eggs are very resistant to most environmental factors and can last for years until the proper conditions enable them to mature. Whipworms are seldom seen in the stool.

Intestinal parasites are more prevalent in some areas than others. Climate, soil and contamination are big factors contributing to the incidence of intestinal parasites. Eggs are passed in the stool, lay on the ground and then become infective in a certain number of days. Each of the above worms has a different life cycle. Your best chance of becoming and remaining worm-free is to always pooper-scoop your yard. A fenced-in yard keeps stray dogs out, which is certainly helpful.

I would recommend having a fecal examination on your dog twice a year or more often if there is a problem. If your dog has a positive fecal sample, then he will be given the appropriate medication and you will be asked to bring back another stool sample in a certain period of time (depending on the type of worm) and then be rewormed. This process goes on until he

Whipworms are hard to find, and it is a job best left to a veterinarian. Pictured here are adult whipworms.

has at least two negative samples. The different types of worms require different medications. You will be wasting your money and doing your dog an injustice by buying over-the-counter medication without first consulting your veterinarian.

Roundworm eggs, as would be seen on a fecal evaluation. The eggs must develop for at least 12 days before they are infective.

OTHER INTERNAL PARASITES

Coccidiosis and Giardiasis

These protozoal infections usually affect puppies, especially in places where large numbers of puppies are brought together. Older dogs may harbor these infections but do not show signs unless they are stressed. Symptoms include diarrhea, weight loss and lack of appetite. These infections are not always apparent in the fecal examination.

Tapeworms

Seldom apparent on fecal floatation, they are diagnosed frequently as rice-like segments around the dog's anus and the base of the tail. Tapeworms are long, flat and ribbon like, sometimes several feet in length, and made up of many segments about five-eighths of an inch long. The two most common types of tapeworms found in the dog are:

(1) First the larval form of the flea tapeworm parasite must mature in an intermediate host, the flea, before it can become infective. Your dog acquires this by ingesting the flea through licking and chewing.

(2) Rabbits, rodents and certain large game animals serve as intermediate hosts for other species of tapeworms. If your dog should eat one of these infected hosts, then he can acquire tapeworms.

HEARTWORM DISEASE

This is a worm that resides in the heart and adjacent blood vessels of the lung that produces microfilaria, which circulate in the bloodstream. It is possible for a dog to be infected with

any number of worms from one to a hundred that can be 6 to 14 inches long. It is a life-threatening disease, expensive to treat and easily prevented. Depending on where you live, your veterinarian may recommend a preventive year-round and either an annual or semiannual blood test. The most common preventive is given once a month.

External Parasites

Fleas

These pests are not only the dog's worst enemy but also enemy to the owner's pocketbook. Preventing is less expensive than treating, but regardless I think we'd prefer to spend our money elsewhere. I would guess that the majority of our dogs are allergic to the bite of a flea, and in many cases it only takes one flea bite.

The cat flea is the most common flea of both dogs and cats. Courtesy of Fleabusters, Rx for Fleas, Inc., Fort Lauderdale, Florida.

The protein in the flea's saliva is the culprit. Allergic dogs have a reaction, which usually results in a "hot spot." More than likely such a reaction will involve a trip to the veterinarian for treatment. Yes, prevention is less expensive. Fortunately today there are several good products available.

If there is a flea infestation, no one product is going to correct the problem. Not only will the dog require treatment so will the environment. In general flea collars are not very effective although there is now available an "egg" collar that will kill the eggs on the dog. Dips are the most economical but they are messy. There are some effective shampoos and treatments available through pet shops and veterinarians. An oral tablet arrived on the American market in 1995 and was popular in Europe the previous year. It sterilizes the female flea but will not kill adult fleas. Therefore the tablet, which is given monthly, will decrease the flea population but is not a "cure-all." Those dogs that suffer from flea-bite allergy will still be subjected to the bite

Fleas can cause a serious skin irritation or an allergic reaction in your dog. If your Springer seems to be scratching excessively, check his coat thoroughly for infestation.

111

of the flea. Another popular parasiticide is permethrin, which is applied to the back of the dog in one or two places depending on the dog's weight. This product works as a repellent causing the flea to get "hot feet" and jump off. Do not confuse this product with some of the organophosphates that are also applied to the dog's back.

Some products are not usable on young puppies. Treating fleas should be done under your veterinarian's guidance. Frequently it is necessary to combine products and the layman does not have the knowledge regarding possible toxicities. It is hard to believe but there are a few dogs that do have a natural resistance to fleas. Nevertheless it would be wise to treat all pets at the same time. Don't forget your cats. Cats just love to prowl the neighborhood and consequently return with unwanted guests.

The best way to prevent and eliminate flea infestation is to use a safe insecticide in the house to kill adult fleas and an insect growth regulator to stop the eggs and larvae.

Adult fleas live on the dog but their eggs drop off the dog into the environment. There they go through four larval stages before reaching adulthood, and thereby are able to jump back on the poor unsuspecting dog. The cycle resumes and takes

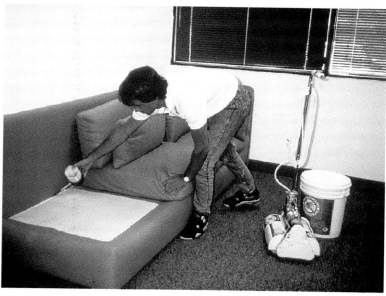

between 21 to 28 days under ideal conditions. There are environmental products available that will kill both the adult fleas and the larvae.

Ticks

Ticks carry Rocky Mountain Spotted Fever, Lyme disease and can cause tick paralysis. They should be removed with tweezers, trying to pull out the head. The jaws carry disease. There is a tick preventive collar that does an excellent job. The ticks automatically back out on those dogs wearing collars.

Sarcoptic Mange

This is a mite that is difficult to find on skin scrapings. The pinnal reflex is a good indicator of this disease. Rub the ends of the pinna (ear) together and the dog will start scratching with his foot. Sarcoptes are highly contagious to other dogs and to humans although they do not live long on humans. They cause intense itching.

Springer Spaniels have a higher risk of infestation when hunting or in the field, because parasites can hide in tall grasses or brush.

Demodectic Mange

This is a mite that is passed from the dam to her puppies. It affects youngsters age three to ten months. Diagnosis is confirmed by skin scraping. Small areas of alopecia around the eyes, lips and/or forelegs become visible. There is little itching unless there is a secondary bacterial infection. Some breeds are afflicted more than others.

Cheyletiella

This causes intense itching and is diagnosed by skin scraping. It lives in the outer layers of the skin of dogs, cats, rabbits and humans. Yellow-gray scales may be found on the back and the rump, top of the head and the nose.

To Breed or Not To Breed

More than likely your breeder has requested that you have your puppy neutered or spayed. Your breeder's request is

Breeding should only be attempted by someone who is conscientious, knowledgeable and willing to take responsibility for the dogs involved and the new puppies.

based on what is healthiest for your dog and what is most beneficial for your breed. Experienced and conscientious breeders devote many years into developing a bloodline. In order to do this, he makes every effort to plan each breeding in regard to conformation, temperament and health. This type of breeder does his best to perform the necessary testing (i.e., OFA, CERF, testing for inherited blood disorders, thyroid, etc.). Testing is expensive and sometimes very disheartening when a favorite dog doesn't pass his health tests. The health history pertains not only to the breeding stock but to the immediate ancestors. Reputable breeders do not want their offspring to be bred indiscriminately. Therefore you may be asked to neuter or spay your puppy. Of course there is always the exception, and your breeder may agree to let you breed your dog under his direct supervision. This is an important concept. More and more effort is being made to breed healthier dogs.

Spay/Neuter

There are numerous benefits of performing this surgery at six months of age. Unspayed females are subject to mammary and ovarian cancer. In order to prevent mammary cancer she must be spayed prior to her first heat cycle. Later in life, an unspayed female may develop a pyometra (an infected uterus), which is definitely life threatening.

Spaying is performed under a general anesthetic and is easy on the young dog. As you might expect it is a little harder on the older dog, but that is no reason to deny her the surgery. The surgery removes the ovaries and uterus. It is important to remove all the ovarian tissue. If some is left behind, she could remain attractive to males. In order to view the ovaries, a reasonably long incision is necessary. An ovariohysterectomy is considered major surgery.

Spaying/neutering is often the best option for your family pet. The health benefits are numerous and it will minimize the risk of certain diseases.

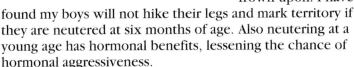

Neutering the male at a young age will inhibit some characteristic male behavior that owners frown upon. I have found my boys will not hike their legs and mark territory if they are neutered at six months of age. Also neutering at a young age has hormonal benefits, lessening the chance of hormonal aggressiveness.

Surgery involves removing the testicles but leaving the scrotum. If there should be a retained testicle, then he definitely needs to be neutered before the age of two or three years. Retained testicles can develop into cancer. Unneutered males are at risk for testicular cancer, perineal fistulas, perianal tumors and fistulas and prostatic disease.

Intact males and females are prone to housebreaking accidents. Females urinate frequently before, during and after heat cycles, and males tend to mark territory if there is a female in heat. Males may show the same behavior if there is a visiting dog or guests.

Surgery involves a sterile operating procedure equivalent to human surgery. The incision site is shaved, surgically scrubbed and draped. The veterinarian wears a sterile surgical gown, cap, mask and gloves. Anesthesia should be monitored by a registered technician. It is customary for the veterinarian to recommend a pre-anesthetic blood screening, looking for metabolic problems and a ECG rhythm strip to check for normal heart function. Today anesthetics are equal to human anesthetics, which enables your dog to walk out of the clinic the same day as surgery.

Some folks worry about their dog gaining weight after being neutered or spayed. This is usually not the case. It is true that some dogs may be

All Springer Spaniel puppies are cute, but not all are of breeding quality. Reputable breeders will often sell pet-quality pups on the condition that they are spayed or neutered.

Proper nutrition is an important key to maintaining your dog's health and avoiding many medical problems that might occur. less active so they could develop a problem, but my own dogs are just as active as they were before surgery. I have a hard time keeping weight on them. However, if your dog should begin to gain, then you need to decrease his food and see to it that he gets a little more exercise.

MEDICAL PROBLEMS

Anal Sacs

These are small sacs on either side of the rectum that can cause the dog discomfort when they are full. They should empty when the dog has a bowel movement. Symptoms of inflammation or impaction are excessive licking under the tail and/or a bloody or sticky discharge from the anal area. Breeders like myself recommend emptying the sacs on a regular schedule when bathing the dog. Many veterinarians prefer this isn't done unless there are symptoms. You can express the sacs by squeezing the two sacs (at the five and seven o'clock positions) in and up toward the anus. Take precautions not to get in the way of the foul-smelling fluid that is expressed. Some dogs object to this procedure so it would be wise to have someone hold the head. Scooting is caused by anal-sac irritation and not worms.

Colitis

The stool may be frank blood or blood tinged and is the result of inflammation of the colon. Colitis, sometimes intermittent, can be the result of stress, undiagnosed whipworms, or perhaps idiopathic (no explainable reason). I have had several dogs prone to this disorder. They felt fine and were willing to eat but would have intermittent bloody stools. If this in an ongoing problem, you should probably feed a diet higher in fiber. Seek professional help if your dog feels poorly and/or the condition persists.

Conjunctivitis

Many breeds are prone to this problem. The conjunctiva is the pink tissue that lines the inner surface of the eyeball except the clear, transparent cornea. Irritating substances such as bacteria, foreign matter or chemicals can cause it to become reddened and swollen. It is important to keep any hair trimmed from around the eyes. Long hair stays damp and aggravates the problem. Keep the eyes cleaned with warm water and wipe away any matter that has accumulated in the corner of the eyes. If the condition persists, you should see your veterinarian. This problem goes hand in hand with keratoconjunctivitis sicca.

Your Springer Spaniel's eyes should be dark and clear, without any signs of redness or irritation.

Ear Infection

Otitis externa is an inflammation of the external ear canal that begins at the outside opening of the ear and extends inward to the eardrum. Dogs with pendulous ears are prone to this disease, but isn't it interesting that breeds with upright ears also have a high incidence of problems? Allergies, food and inhalent, along with hormonal problems, such as hypothyroidism, are major contributors to the disease. For those dogs which have recurring problems you need to investigate the underlying cause if you hope to cure them.

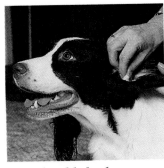

You should check your Springer's ears regularly and use a cotton ball to keep them clean and free of waxy build-up.

I recommend that you are careful never to get water into the ears. Water provides a great medium for bacteria to grow. If your dog swims or you inadvertently get water into his ears, then use a drying agent. An at-home preparation would be to use equal parts of three-percent hydrogen peroxide and 70-percent rubbing alcohol. Another preparation is equal parts of white vinegar and water. Your veterinarian alternatively can provide a suitable product. When cleaning the ears, be careful of using cotton tip applicators since they make it easy to pack debris down into the canal. Only clean what you can see.

If your dog has an ongoing infection, don't be surprised if your veterinarian recommends sedating him and flushing his ears with a bulb syringe. Sometimes this needs to be done a few times to get the ear clean. The ear must be clean so that medication can come in contact with the canal. Be prepared to return for rechecks until the infection is gone. This may involve more flushings if the ears are very bad.

For chronic or recurring cases, your veterinarian may recommend thyroid testing, etc., and a hypoallergenic diet for a trial period of 10 to 12 weeks. Depending on your dog, it may be a good idea to see a dermatologist. Ears shouldn't be taken lightly. If the condition gets out of hand, then surgery may be necessary. Please ask your veterinarian to explain proper ear maintenance for your dog.

Flea Bite Allergy

This is the result of a hypersensitivity to the bite of a flea and its saliva. It only takes one bite to cause the dog to chew or scratch himself raw. Your dog may need medical attention to ease his discomfort. You need to clip the hair around the "hot spot" and wash it with a mild soap and water and you may need to do this daily if the area weeps. Apply an antibiotic anti-inflammatory product. Hot spots can occur from other trauma, such as grooming.

Interdigital Cysts

Check for these on your dog's feet if he shows signs of lameness. They are frequently associated with staph infections and can be quite painful. A home remedy is to soak the infected foot in a solution of a half teaspoon of bleach in a couple of quarts of water. Do this two to three times a day for a couple of days. Check with your veterinarian for an alternative remedy; antibiotics usually work well. If there is a recurring problem, surgery may be required.

Lameness

It may only be an interdigital cyst or it could be a mat between the toes, especially if your dog licks his feet. Sometimes it is hard to determine which leg is affected. If he is holding up his leg, then you need to see your veterinarian.

Skin

Frequently poor skin is the result of an allergy to fleas, an inhalant allergy or food allergy. These types of problems usually result in a staph dermatitis. Dogs with food allergy usually show signs of severe itching and scratching. However, I have had some dogs

Regular medical care is just as important for the adult Springer as it is for the puppy. Vaccination boosters and physical exams are part of your dog's lifelong maintenance.

The Springer is an athletic dog that should move freely and easily. Any signs of lameness should be checked by your veterinarian immediately.

with food allergies that never once itched. Their only symptom was swelling of the ears with no ear infection. Food allergy may result in recurrent bacterial skin and ear infections. Your veterinarian or dermatologist will recommend a good restricted diet. It is not wise for you to hit and miss with different dog foods. Many of the diets offered over the counter are not the hypoallergenic diet you are led to believe. Dogs acquire allergies through exposure.

Inhalant allergies result in atopy, which causes licking of the feet, scratching the body and rubbing the muzzle. It may be seasonable. Your veterinarian or dermatologist can perform intradermal testing for inhalant allergies. If your dog should test positive, then a vaccine may be prepared. The results are very satisfying.

Tonsillitis

Usually young dogs have a higher incidence of this problem than the older ones. The older dogs have built up resistance. It is very contagious. Sometimes it is difficult to determine if it is tonsillitis or kennel cough since the symptoms are similar. Symptoms include fever, poor eating, swallowing with difficulty and retching up a white, frothy mucus.

121

DENTAL CARE for Your Dog's Life

So you've got a new puppy! You also have a new set of puppy teeth in your household. Anyone who has ever raised a puppy is abundantly aware of these new teeth. Your puppy will chew anything it can reach, chase your shoelaces, and play "tear the rag" with any piece of clothing it can find. When puppies are newly born, they have no teeth. At about four weeks of age, puppies of most breeds begin to develop their deciduous or baby teeth. They begin eating semi-solid food, fighting and biting with their litter mates, and learning discipline from their mother. As their new teeth come in, they inflict more pain on their mother's breasts, so her feeding sessions become less frequent and shorter. By six or eight weeks, the mother will start growling to warn her pups when they are fighting too roughly or hurting her as they nurse too much with their new teeth.

Puppies need to chew. It is a necessary part of their physical and mental development. They develop

Your Springer will be happier and his teeth will be healthier if you give him a giant-sized POPpup™ to chew on. Every POPpup™ is 100% edible and enhanced with dog-friendly ingredients like liver, cheese, spinach, chicken, carrots or potatoes.

You and your Springer Spaniel can enjoy hours of fun with a Nylafloss®. It's a great tug toy (when you initiate and end the game!), your dog can retrieve it and it does wonders for your Springer's dental health by massaging his gums and literally flossing between his teeth.

muscles and necessary life skills as they drag objects around, fight over possession, and vocalize alerts and warnings. Puppies chew on things to explore their world. They are using their sense of taste to determine what is food and what is not. How else can they tell an electrical cord from a lizard? At about four months of age, most puppies begin shedding their baby teeth. Often these teeth need some help to come out and make way for the permanent teeth. The incisors (front teeth) will be replaced first. Then, the adult canine or fang teeth erupt. When the baby tooth is not shed before the permanent tooth comes in, veterinarians call it a retained deciduous tooth. This condition will often cause gum infections by trapping hair and debris between the permanent tooth and the retained baby tooth. Nylafloss® is an excellent device for puppies to use. They can toss it, drag it, and chew on the many surfaces it presents. The baby teeth can catch in the nylon material, aiding in their removal. Puppies that have adequate chew toys will have less destructive behavior, develop more physically, and have less chance of retained deciduous teeth.

During the first year, your dog should be seen by your veterinarian at regular intervals. Your veterinarian will let you know when to bring in your puppy for vaccinations and parasite examinations. At each visit, your veterinarian should inspect the lips, teeth, and mouth as part of a complete physical examination. You should take some part in the maintenance of your dog's oral health. You should examine your dog's mouth weekly throughout his first year to *A thorough oral examination of your English Springer Spaniel's mouth, teeth and gums should be part of his annual check-up.* make sure there are no sores, foreign objects, tooth problems, etc. If your dog drools excessively, shakes its head, or has bad breath, consult your veterinarian. By the time your dog is six months old, the permanent teeth are all in and plaque can start to accumulate on the tooth surfaces. This is when your dog needs to develop good dental-care habits to prevent calculus build-up on its teeth. Brushing is best. That is a fact that cannot be denied. However, some dogs do not like their teeth brushed regularly, or you may not be able to accomplish the task. In that case, you should consider a product that will help prevent plaque and calculus build-up.

The Plaque Attackers® and Galileo Bone® are other excellent choices for the first three years of a dog's life. Their shapes make them interesting for the dog. As the dog chews on them, the solid polyurethane massages the gums which improves the blood circulation to the periodontal tissues. Projections on the chew devices increase the surface and are in contact with the

Puppies need to chew as part of their physical and mental development. Give your puppies something safe and fun, like the Nylabone® Dental Dinosaur™ to gnaw on.

tooth for more efficient cleaning. The unique shape and consistency prevent your dog from exerting excessive force on his own teeth or from breaking off pieces of the bone. If your dog is an aggressive chewer or weighs more than 55 pounds (25 kg), you should consider giving him a Nylabone®, the most durable chew product on the market.

The Gumabones®, made by the Nylabone Company, is constructed of strong polyurethane, which is softer than nylon. Less powerful chewers prefer the Gumabones® to the Nylabones®. A super option for your dog is the Hercules Bone®, a uniquely shaped bone named after the great Olympian for its exception strength. Like all Nylabone products, they are specially scented to make them attractive to your dog. Ask your veterinarian about these bones and he will validate the good doctor's prescription: Nylabones® not only give your dog a good chewing workout but also help to save your dog's teeth (and even his life, as it protects him from possible fatal periodontal diseases).

By the time dogs are four years old, 75% of them have periodontal disease. It is the most common infection in dogs. Yearly examinations by your veterinarian are essential to maintaining your dog's good health. If your

Your English Springer Spaniel needs a chew device that's up to his standard, and with the Hercules® bone, he's got one. The unique design of the Hercules® enables aggressive chewers to grab on to it anywhere for a solid, satisfying chew.

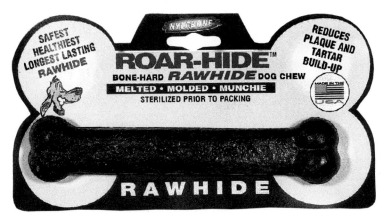

To combat boredom and relieve your Springer Spaniel's natural desire to chew, there's nothing better than a Roar-Hide™. Unlike common rawhide, this bone won't turn into a gooey mess when chewed on, so your dog won't choke on small pieces of it. The Roar-Hide™ is completely edible, high in protein and low in fat.

veterinarian detects periodontal disease, he or she may recommend a prophylactic cleaning. To do a thorough cleaning, it will be necessary to put your dog under anesthesia. With modern gas anesthetics and monitoring equipment, the procedure is pretty safe. Your veterinarian will scale the teeth with an ultrasound scaler or hand instrument. This removes the calculus from the teeth. If there are calculus deposits below the gum line, the veterinarian will plane the roots to make them smooth. After all of the calculus has been removed, the teeth are polished with pumice in a polishing cup. If any medical or surgical treatment is needed, it is done at this time. The final step would be fluoride treatment and your follow-up treatment at home. If the periodontal disease is advanced, the veterinarian may prescribe a medicated mouth rinse or antibiotics for use at home. Make sure your dog has safe, clean and attractive chew toys and treats. Chooz® treats are another way of using a consumable treat to help keep your dog's teeth clean.

Rawhide is the most popular of all materials for a dog to chew. This has never been good news to dog owners, because rawhide is inherently very dangerous for dogs. Thousands of dogs have died from rawhide, having swallowed the hide after

it has become soft and mushy, only to cause stomach and intestinal blockage. A new rawhide product on the market has finally solved the problem of rawhide: molded Roar-Hide® from Nylabone. These are composed of processed, cut up, and melted American rawhide injected into your dog's favorite shape: a dog bone. These dog-safe devices smell and taste like rawhide but don't break up. The ridges on the bones help to fight tartar build-up on the teeth and they last ten times longer than the usual rawhide chews.

A Gumabone® Frisbee™* is a great toy for games of fetch with your English Springer Spaniel. It's flexible enough for your dog to carry, and the bone on top makes it easy to pick up. *The trademark Frisbee is used under license from Mattel, Inc., CA, USA.

As your dog ages, professional examination and cleaning should become more frequent. The mouth should be inspected at least once a year. Your veterinarian may recommend visits every six months. In the geriatric patient, organs such as the heart, liver, and kidneys do not function as well as when they were young. Your veterinarian will probably want to test these organs' functions prior to using general anesthesia for dental cleaning. If your dog is a good chewer and you work closely with your veterinarian, your dog can keep all of its teeth all of its life. However, as your dog ages, his sense of smell, sight, and taste will diminish. He may not have the desire to chase, trap or chew his toys. He will also not have the energy to chew for long periods, as arthritis and periodontal disease make chewing painful. This will leave you with more responsibility for keeping his teeth clean and healthy. The dog that would not let you brush his teeth at one year of age, may let you brush his teeth now that he is ten years old.

If your Springer would rather chew than do anything else, the Gumabone® is the device for him. Offer him a Gumabone® made of non-toxic, durable polyurethane, to sink his teeth into.

If you train your dog with good chewing habits as a puppy, he will have healthier teeth throughout his life.

129

BEHAVIOR and Canine Communication

Studies of the human/animal bond point out the importance of the unique relationships that exist between people and their pets. Those of us who share our lives with pets understand the special part they play through companionship, service and protection. For many, the pet/owner bond goes beyond simple companionship; pets are often considered members of the family. A leading pet food manufacturer recently conducted a nationwide survey of pet owners to gauge just how important pets were in their lives. Here's what they found:

Children make great playmates for energetic puppies and caring for them teaches a child responsibility and respect for animals. This is Glenn Kichler with his Springer buddies.

- 76 percent allow their pets to sleep on their beds
- 78 percent think of their pets as their children
- 84 percent display photos of their pets, mostly in their homes
- 84 percent think that their pets react to their own emotions
- 100 percent talk to their pets
- 97 percent think that their pets understand what they're saying

Are you surprised?

Senior citizens show more concern for their own eating habits when they have the responsibility of feeding a dog. Seeing that their dog is routinely exercised encourages the owner to think of schedules that otherwise may seem unimportant to the senior citizen. The older owner may be arthritic and feeling poorly but with responsibility for his dog he has a reason to get up and get moving. It is a big plus if his dog is an attention seeker who will demand such from his owner.

Dogs are a very important part of their owner's lives, and the bond between humans and animals is a strong one.

Over the last couple of decades, it has been shown that pets relieve the stress of those who lead busy lives. Owning a pet has been known to lessen the occurrence of heart attack and stroke.

Many single folks thrive on the companionship of a dog. Lifestyles are very different from a long time ago, and today more individuals seek the single life. However, they receive fulfillment from owning a dog.

Most likely the majority of our dogs live in family environments. The companionship they provide is well worth the effort involved. In my opinion, every child should have the opportunity to have a family dog. Dogs teach responsibility through understanding their care, feelings and even respecting

Many people thrive on the devoted companionship an English Springer Spaniel can provide.

their life cycles. Frequently those children who have not been exposed to dogs grow up afraid of dogs, which isn't good. Dogs sense timidity and some will take advantage of the situation.

Today more dogs are serving as service dogs. Since the origination of the Seeing Eye dogs years ago, we now have trained hearing dogs. Also dogs are trained to provide service for the handicapped and are able to perform many different tasks for their owners. Search and Rescue dogs, with their handlers, are sent throughout the world to assist in recovery of disaster victims. They are life savers.

Therapy dogs are very popular with nursing homes, and some hospitals even allow them to visit. The inhabitants truly look forward to their visits. I have taken a couple of my dogs visiting and left in tears when I saw the response of the patients. They wanted and were allowed to have my dogs in their beds to hold and love.

Nationally there is a Pet Awareness Week to educate students and others about the value and basic care of our pets. Many countries take an even greater interest in their pets than Americans do. In those countries the pets are allowed to accompany their owners into restaurants and shops, etc. In the U.S. this freedom is only available to our service dogs. Even so we think very highly of the human/animal bond.

Although some traits are inherited within a breed, every Springer is an individual with his own personality.

CANINE BEHAVIOR

Canine behavior problems are the number-one reason for pet owners to dispose of their dogs, either through new homes, humane shelters or euthanasia. Unfortunately there are too many owners who are unwilling to devote the necessary time to properly train their dogs. On the other hand, there are those who not only are concerned about inherited health problems but are also aware of the dog's mental stability.

You may realize that a breed and his group relatives (i.e., sporting, hounds, etc.) show tendencies to behavioral characteristics. An experienced breeder can acquaint you with his breed's personality. Unfortunately many breeds are labeled with poor temperaments when actually the breed as a whole is not affected but only a small percentage of individuals within the breed.

If the breed in question is very popular, then of course there may be a higher number of unstable dogs. Do not label a breed good or bad. I know of absolutely awful-tempered dogs within one of our most popular, lovable breeds.

Inheritance and environment contribute to the dog's

behavior. Some naive people suggest inbreeding as the cause of bad temperaments. Inbreeding only results in poor behavior if the ancestors carry the trait. If there are excellent temperaments behind the dogs, then inbreeding will promote good temperaments in the offspring. Did you ever consider that inbreeding is what sets the characteristics of a breed? A purebred dog is the end result of inbreeding. This does not spare the mixed-breed dog from the same problems. Mixed-breed dogs frequently are the offspring of purebred dogs.

When planning a breeding, I like to observe the potential stud and his offspring in the show ring. If I see unruly behavior, I try to look into it further. I want to know if it is genetic or environmental, due to the lack of training and socialization. A good breeder will avoid breeding mentally unsound dogs.

Your puppy's relationship with his littermates is an essential one. He will learn to interact with other dogs by playing with his siblings.

Not too many decades ago most of our dogs led a different lifestyle than what is prevalent today. Usually mom stayed home so the dog had human companionship and someone to discipline it if needed. Not much was expected from the dog. Today's mom works and everyone's life is at a much faster pace.

The dog may have to adjust to being a "weekend" dog. The family is gone all day during the week, and the dog is left to his own devices for entertainment. Some dogs sleep all day waiting for their family to come home and others become wigwam wreckers if given the opportunity. Crates do ensure the safety of the dog and the house. However, he could become a physically and emotionally cripple if he doesn't get enough exercise and attention. We still appreciate and want the companionship of our dogs although we expect more from them. In many cases we tend to forget dogs are just that—*dogs* not human beings.

To be properly sociaized, your Springer puppy should meet as many different people as possible while growing up.

I own several dogs who are left crated during the day but I do try to make time for them in the evenings and on the weekends. Also we try to do something together before I leave for work. Maybe it helps them to have the companionship of other dogs. They accept their crates as their personal "houses" and seem to be content with their routine and thrive on trying their best to please me.

SOCIALIZING AND TRAINING

Many prospective puppy buyers lack experience regarding the proper socialization and training needed to develop the type of pet we all desire. In the first 18 months, training does take some work. Trust me, it is easier to start proper training before there is a problem that needs to be corrected.

The initial work begins with the breeder. The breeder should start socializing the puppy at five to six weeks of age and cannot let up. Human socializing is critical up through 12 weeks of age and likewise important during the following months. The litter should be left together during the first few weeks but it is necessary to separate them by ten weeks of age. Leaving them together after that time will increase competition for litter dominance. If puppies are not socialized with people by 12 weeks of age, they will be timid in later life.

The eight- to ten-week age period is a fearful time for puppies. They need to be handled very gently around children and adults. There should be no harsh discipline during this time. Starting at 14 weeks of age, the puppy begins the juvenile period, which ends when he reaches sexual maturity around six to 14 months of age. During the juvenile period he needs to be introduced to strangers (adults, children and other dogs) on the home property. At sexual maturity he will begin to bark at strangers and become more protective. Males start to lift their legs to urinate but if you desire you can inhibit this behavior by walking your boy on leash away from trees, shrubs, fences, etc.

Perhaps you are thinking about an older puppy. You need to

Puppies need proper training and socialization from the very beginning to become a welcomed and valued member of your household.

English Springer Spaniels are highly intelligent dogs that can be taught to excel at many different activities when properly trained. This Springer conquers the high jump.

inquire about the puppy's social experience. If he has lived in a kennel, he may have a hard time adjusting to people and environmental stimuli. Assuming he has had a good social upbringing, there are advantages to an older puppy.

Training includes puppy kindergarten and a minimum of one to two basic training classes. During these classes you will learn how to dominate your youngster. This is especially important if you own a large breed of dog. It is somewhat harder, if not nearly impossible, for some owners to be the Alpha figure when their dog towers over them. You will be taught how to properly restrain your dog. This concept is important. Again it puts you in the Alpha position. All dogs need to be restrained many times during their lives. Believe it or not, some of our worst offenders are the eight-week-old puppies that are brought to our clinic. They need to be gently restrained for a nail trim but the way they carry on you would think we were killing them. In comparison, their vaccination is a "piece of cake." When we ask dogs to do something that is not agreeable to them, then their worst comes out. Life will be easier for your dog if you expose him at a young age to the necessities of life—proper behavior and restraint.

UNDERSTANDING THE DOG'S LANGUAGE

Most authorities agree that the dog is a descendent of the wolf. The dog and wolf have similar traits. For instance both are pack oriented and prefer not to be isolated for long periods of time. Another characteristic is that the dog, like the wolf, looks to the leader—Alpha—for direction. Both the wolf and the dog communicate through body language, not only within their pack but with outsiders.

Every pack has an Alpha figure. The dog looks to you, or should look to you, to be that leader. If your dog doesn't receive the proper training and guidance, he very well may replace you as Alpha. This would be a serious problem and is certainly a disservice to your dog.

Eye contact is one way the Alpha wolf keeps order within his pack. You are Alpha so you must establish eye contact with your puppy. Obviously your puppy will have to look at you. Practice eye contact even if you need to hold his head for five to ten seconds at a time. You can give him a treat as a reward. Make sure your eye contact is gentle and not threatening. Later, if he has been naughty, it is permissible to give him a long, penetrating look. I caution you there are some older dogs that never learned eye contact as puppies and cannot accept eye contact. You should avoid eye contact with these dogs since they feel threatened and will retaliate as such.

BODY LANGUAGE

The play bow, when the forequarters are down and the hindquarters are elevated, is an invitation to play. Puppies play fight, which helps them learn the acceptable limits of biting. This is necessary for later in their lives. Nevertheless, an owner may be falsely reassured by the playful nature of his dog's

This Springer Spaniel shows that he is submissive to his master by laying on his side, belly exposed—and receives a tummy rub as a reward!

aggression. Playful aggression toward another dog or human may be an indication of serious aggression in the future. Owners should never play fight or play tug-of-war with any dog that is inclined to be dominant. Signs of submission are:

1. Avoids eye contact.
2. Active submission—the dog crouches down, ears back and the tail is lowered.
3. Passive submission—the dog rolls on his side with his hindlegs in the air and frequently urinates.

Dogs are popular because of their sociable nature, but a dog that displays dominance over his family will be difficult to train and hard to control.

Signs of dominance are:

1. Makes eye contact.
2. Stands with ears up, tail up and the hair raised on his neck.
3. Shows dominance over another dog by standing at right angles over it.

Dominant dogs tend to behave in characteristic ways such as:

1. The dog may be unwilling to move from his place (i.e., reluctant to give up the sofa if the owner wants to sit there).
2. He may not part with toys or objects in his mouth and may show possessiveness with his food bowl.
3. He may not respond quickly to commands.
4. He may be disagreeable for grooming and dislikes to be petted.

Dogs are popular because of their sociable nature. Those that have contact with humans during the first 12 weeks of life regard them as a member of their own species—their pack. All dogs have the potential for both dominant and submissive behavior. Only through experience and training do they learn to whom it is appropriate to show which behavior. Not all dogs are concerned with dominance but owners need to be aware of that potential. It is wise for the owner to establish his dominance early on.

A human can express dominance or submission toward a dog in the following ways:

1. Meeting the dog's gaze signals dominance. Averting the gaze signals submission. If the dog growls or threatens, averting the gaze is the first avoiding action to take—it may prevent attack. It is important to establish eye contact in the puppy. The older dog that has not been exposed to eye contact may see it as a threat and will not be willing to submit.

2. Being taller than the dog signals dominance; being lower signals submission. This is why, when attempting to make friends with a strange dog or catch the runaway, one should kneel down to his level. Some owners see their dogs become dominant when allowed on the furniture or on the bed. Then he is at the owner's level.

An unwillingness to give up his toys may signal that your dog is displaying dominant tendencies. Your Springer must always know that you are the boss.

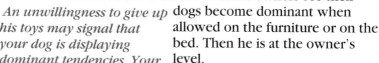

3. An owner can gain dominance by ignoring all the dog's social initiatives. The owner pays attention to the dog only when he obeys a command.

No dog should be allowed to achieve dominant status over any adult or child. Ways of preventing are as follows:

1. Handle the puppy gently, especially during the three- to four-month period.

2. Let the children and adults handfeed him and teach him to take food without lunging or grabbing.

3. Do not allow him to chase children or joggers.

4. Do not allow him to jump on people or mount their legs. Even females may be inclined to mount. It is not only a male habit.

5. Do not allow him to growl for any reason.

6. Don't participate in wrestling or tug-of-war games.

7. Don't physically punish puppies for aggressive behavior. Restrain him from repeating the infraction and teach an alternative behavior. Dogs should earn everything they receive from their owners. This would include sitting to receive petting or treats, sitting before going out the

Teach your Springer how you want him to behave. Practicing training and obedience exercises will further demonstrate your dominance. door and sitting to receive the collar and leash. These types of exercises reinforce the owner's dominance.

Young children should never be left alone with a dog. It is important that children learn some basic obedience commands so they have some control over the dog. They will gain the respect of their dog.

FEAR

One of the most common problems dogs experience is being fearful. Some dogs are more afraid than others. On the lesser side, which is sometimes humorous to watch, my dog can be afraid of a strange object. He acts silly when something is out of place in the house. I call his problem perceptive intelligence. He realizes the abnormal within his known environment. He does not react the same way in strange environments since he does not know what is normal.

On the more serious side is a fear of people. This can result in backing off, seeking his own space and saying "leave me alone" or it can result in an aggressive behavior that may lead to challenging the person. Respect that the dog wants to be left alone and give him time to come forward. If you approach the cornered dog, he may resort to snapping. If you leave him alone, he may decide to come forward, which should be rewarded with a treat. Years ago we had a dog that behaved in this manner. We coaxed people to stop by the house and make friends with our fearful dog. She learned to take the treats and after weeks of work she overcame her suspicions and made friends more readily.

Some dogs may initially be too fearful to take treats. In these cases it is helpful to make sure the dog hasn't eaten for about 24 hours. Being a little hungry encourages him to accept the treats, especially if they are of the "gourmet" variety. I have a dog that worries about strangers since people seldom stop by my house. Over the years she has learned a cue and jumps up quickly to visit anyone sitting on the sofa. She learned by herself that all guests on the sofa were to be trusted friends. I think she felt more comfortable with them being at her level, rather than towering over her.

Dogs can be afraid of numerous things, including loud noises and thunderstorms. Invariably the owner rewards (by comforting) the dog when it shows signs of fearfulness. I had a terrible problem with my favorite dog in the Utility obedience class. Not only was he intimidated in the class but he was afraid of noise and afraid of displeasing me. Frequently he would knock down the bar jump, which clattered dreadfully. I gave him credit because he continued to try to clear it, although he was terribly scared. I finally learned to "reward" him every time he knocked down the jump. I would jump up and down, clap my hands and tell him how great he was. My psychology worked, he relaxed and eventually cleared the jump with ease. When your dog is frightened, direct his attention to something else and act happy. Don't dwell on his fright.

AGGRESSION

Some different types of aggression are: predatory, defensive, dominance, possessive, protective, fear induced, noise provoked, "rage" syndrome (unprovoked aggression), maternal and aggression directed toward other dogs. Aggression is the most common behavioral problem encountered. Protective breeds are expected to be more aggressive than others but with the proper upbringing they can make very dependable companions. You need to be able to read your dog.

Many factors contribute to aggression including genetics and environment. An improper environment, which may include the living conditions, lack of social life, excessive punishment, being attacked or frightened by an aggressive dog, etc., can all influence a dog's behavior. Even spoiling him and giving too much praise may be detrimental. Isolation and the lack of human contact or exposure to frequent teasing by children or adults also can ruin a good dog.

Introduce your puppy to as many people and situations as possible if he seems to be exhibiting fearful behavior. If his fear is not dealt with, he may turn aggressive.

Lack of direction, fear, or confusion lead to aggression in those dogs that are so inclined. Any obedience exercise, even the sit and down, can direct the dog and overcome fear and/or confusion. Every dog should learn these

commands as a youngster, and there should be periodic reinforcement.

When a dog is showing signs of aggression, you should speak calmly (no screaming or hysterics) and firmly give a command that he understands, such as the sit. As soon as your dog obeys, you have assumed your dominant position. Aggression presents a problem because there may be danger to others. Sometimes it is an emotional issue. Owners may consciously or unconsciously encourage their dog's aggression. Other owners show responsibility by accepting the problem and taking measures to keep it under control. The owner is responsible for his dog's actions, and it is not wise to take a chance on someone being bitten, especially a child. Euthanasia is the solution for some owners and in severe cases this may be the best choice. However, few dogs are that dangerous and very few are that much of a

Well-socialized puppies should be able to play with each other without showing fear or aggression.

Dogs like the English Springer Spaniel possess instinctive behaviors. Proper training is mportant to ensure that these tendencies are displayed in appropriate ways.

threat to their owners. If caution is exercised and professional help is gained early on, then I surmise most cases can be controlled.

Some authorities recommend feeding a lower protein (less than 20 percent) diet. They believe this can aid in reducing aggression. If the dog loses weight, then vegetable oil can be added. Veterinarians and behaviorists are having some success with pharmacology. In many cases treatment is possible and can improve the situation.

If you have done everything according to "the book" regarding training and socializing and are still having a behavior problem, don't procrastinate. It is important that the problem gets attention before it is out of hand. It is estimated that 20 percent of a veterinarian's time may be devoted to dealing with problems before they become so intolerable that the dog is separated from its home and owner. If your veterinarian isn't able to help, he should refer you to a behaviorist.

PROBLEMS

Barking

This is a habit that shouldn't be encouraged. Over the years I've had new puppy owners call to say that their dog hasn't learned to bark. I assure them they are indeed fortunate but not to worry. Some owners desire their dog to bark so as to be a watchdog. In my experience, most dogs will bark when a stranger comes to the door.

The new puppy frequently barks or whines in the crate in his strange environment and the owner reinforces the puppy's bad behavior by going to him during the night. This is a no-no. I tell my new owners to smack the top of the crate and say "quiet" in a loud, firm voice. The puppies don't like to hear the loud noise of the crate being banged. If the barking is sleep-interrupting, then the owner should take crate and pup to the bedroom for a few days until the puppy becomes adjusted to his new environment. Otherwise ignore the barking during the night.

Dogs often jump up as a sign of affection. However, your Springer must learn that not everyone will appreciate paw prints on their clothes!

Barking can be an inherited problem or a bad habit learned through the environment. It takes dedication to stop the barking. Attention should be paid to the cause of the barking. Does the dog seek attention, does he need to go out, is it feeding time, is it occurring when he is left alone, is it a protective bark, etc.? Presently I have a ten-week-old puppy that is a real loud mouth, which I am sure is an inherited tendency. Both her mother and especially her grandmother are overzealous barkers but fortunately have mellowed with the years. My young puppy is corrected with a firm "no" and gentle shaking and she is responding. When barking presents a problem for you, try to stop it as soon as it begins.

There are electronic collars available that are supposed to curb barking. Personally I have not had experience with them. There are some disadvantages to to the collar. If the dog is barking out of excitement, punishment is not the appropriate treatment. Presumably there is the chance the collar could be activated by other stimuli and thereby punish the dog when it is not barking. Should you decide to use one, then you should

seek help from a person with experience with that type of collar. In my opinion I feel the root of the problem needs to be investigated and corrected.

In extreme circumstances (usually when there is a problem with the neighbors), some people have resorted to having their dogs debarked. I caution you that the dog continues to bark but usually only a squeaking sound is heard. Frequently the vocal cords grow back. Probably the biggest concern is that the dog can be left with scar tissue which can narrow the opening to the trachea.

Jumping Up

Personally, I am not thrilled when other dogs jump on me but I have hurt feelings if they don't! I do encourage my own dogs to jump on me, on command. Some do and some don't. In my opinion, a dog that jumps up is a happy

Springer Spaniels love "people food," but must learn to never just help themselves! Good manners is a necessary quality in your dog.

dog. Nevertheless few guests appreciate dogs jumping on them. Clothes get footprinted and/or snagged.

I am a believer in allowing the puppy to jump up during his first few weeks. In my opinion if you correct him too soon and at the wrong age you may intimidate him. Consequently he could be timid around humans later in his life. However, there will come a time, probably around four months of age, that he needs to know when it is okay to jump and when he is to show off good manners by sitting instead.

Some authorities never allow jumping. If you are irritated by your dog jumping up on you, then you should discourage it from the beginning. A larger breed of dog can cause harm to a senior citizen. Some are quite fragile. It may not take much to cause a topple that could break a hip.

How do you correct the problem? All family members need to participate in teaching the puppy to sit as soon as he starts to jump up. The sit must be practiced every time he starts to jump up. Don't forget to praise him for his good behavior.

It is fine to give your dog an occasional treat, but don't do it too often or your Springer may lose interest in eating his regular meals.

If an older dog has acquired the habit, grasp his paws and squeeze tightly. Give a firm "No." He'll soon catch on. Remember the entire family must take part. Each time you allow him to jump up you go back a step in training.

Biting

All puppies bite and try to chew on your fingers, toes, arms, etc. This is the time to teach them to be gentle and not bite hard. Put your fingers in your puppy's mouth and if he bites too hard then say "easy" and let him know he's hurting you. I squeal and act like I have been seriously hurt. If the puppy plays too rough and doesn't respond to your corrections, then he needs "Time Out" in his crate. You should be particularly careful with young children and puppies who still have their deciduous (baby) teeth. Those teeth are like needles and can leave little scars on youngsters. My adult daughter still has a small scar on her face from when she teased an eight-week-old puppy as an eight-year-old.

Springer Spaniels love to use their noses, but excessive digging can be a sign of boredom or stress. Keep your dog occupied with exercise and activities.

Biting in the more mature dog is something that should be prevented at all costs. Should it occur I would quickly let him know in no uncertain terms that biting will not be tolerated. When biting is directed toward another dog (dog fight), don't get in the middle of it. On more than one occasion I have had to separate a couple of my dogs and usually was in the middle of that one last lunge by the offender. Some authorities recommend breaking up a fight by elevating the hind legs. This would only be possible if there was a person for each dog. Obviously it would be hard to fight with the hind legs off the ground. A dog bite is serious and should be given attention. Wash the bite with soap and water and contact your doctor. It is important to know the status of the offender's rabies vaccination.

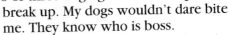

I have several dogs that are sensitive to having mats combed out of their coats and eventually they have had enough. They give fair warning by turning and acting like they would like to nip my offending fingers. However, one verbal warning from me says, "I'm sorry, don't you dare think about biting me and please let me carefully comb just a little bit more." I have owned a minimum of 30 dogs and raised many more puppies and have yet to have one of my dogs bite me except during that last lunge in the two or three dog fights I felt compelled to break up. My dogs wouldn't dare bite me. They know who is boss.

Because the English Springer Spaniel is so eager to please, he is one of the most trainable breeds in existence.

This is not always the case for other owners. I do not wish to frighten you but when biting occurs you should seek professional help at once. On the other hand you must not let your dog intimidate you and be so afraid of a bite that you can't discipline him. Professional help through your veterinarian, dog trainer and/or behaviorist can give you guidance.

Digging

Bored dogs release their frustrations through mischievous behavior such as digging. For the life of me I do not understand why people own dogs only to keep them outside. Dogs shouldn't be left unattended outside, even if they are in a fenced-in yard. Usually the dog is sent to "jail" (the backyard) because the owner can't tolerate him in the house. The culprit feels socially deprived and needs to be included in the owner's life. The owner has neglected the dog's training. The dog has not developed into the companion we desire. If you are one of these owners, then perhaps it is possible for you to change. Give him another chance. Some owners object to their dog's unkempt coat and doggy odor. See that he is groomed on a regular schedule and look into some training classes.

151

Submissive Urination

This is not a housebreaking problem. It can occur in all breeds and may be more prevalent in some breeds. Usually it occurs in puppies but occasionally it occurs in older dogs and may be in response to physical praise. Try verbal praise or ignoring your dog until after he has had a chance to relieve himself. Scolding will only make the problem worse. Many dogs outgrow this problem.

There are many predicaments your Springer puppy can get into in the great outdoors. Always supervise him closely when outside.

Coprophagia

Also know as stool eating, sometimes occurs without a cause. It may begin with boredom and then becomes a habit that is hard to break. Your best remedy is to keep the puppy on a leash and keep the yard picked up. Then he won't have an opportunity to get in trouble. I do not like to clean up accidents or "poop scoop" the yard in front of puppies. I'm suspicious that some puppies try to help and will clean up the stool before I have a chance. Your veterinarian can dispense a medication that is put on the dog's food that makes the stool taste bitter. Of course this will do little good if your dog cleans up after other dogs.

The Runaway

There is little excuse for a dog to run away since dogs should never be off leash except when supervised in the fenced-in yard.

I receive phone calls on a regular basis from prospective owners that want to purchase a female since a male is inclined to roam. It is true that an intact male is inclined to roam, which is one of the reasons a male should be neutered. However, females will roam also, especially if they are in heat. Regardless, these dogs should never be given this opportunity.

Keep your Springer on-lead when outdoors to prevent him from becoming separated from you.

A few years ago one of our clients elected euthanasia for her elderly dog that radiographically appeared to have an intestinal blockage. The veterinarian suggested it might be a corncob. She assured him that was not possible since they hadn't had any. Apparently he roamed and raided the neighbor's garbage and you guessed it—he had a corncob blocking his intestines. Another dog raided the neighbor's garbage and died from toxins from the garbage.

To give the benefit of the doubt, perhaps your dog escapes or perhaps you are playing with your dog in the yard and he refuses to come when called. You now have a runaway. I have had this happen on a smaller scale in the house and have, even to my embarrassment, witnessed this in the obedience ring.

Help! The first thing to remember is when you finally do catch your naughty dog, you must not discipline him. The reasoning behind this is that it is quite possible there could be a repeat performance, and it would be nice if the next time he would respond to your sweet command.

Always kneel down when trying to catch the runaway. Dogs are afraid of people standing over them. Also it would be helpful to have a treat or a favorite toy to help entice him to your side. After that initial runaway experience, start practicing the recall with your dog. You can let him drag a long line (clothesline) and randomly call him and then reel him in. Let him touch you first. Reaching for the dog can frighten him. Each time he comes you reward him with a treat and eventually he should get the idea that this is a nice experience. The long line prevents him from really getting out of hand. My dogs tend to come promptly within about 3 to 4 feet (out of reach) and then turn tail and run. It's "catch me if you can." At least with the long line you can step on it and stop him.

Food Guarding

If you see signs of your puppy guarding his food, then you should take immediate steps to correct the problem. It is not fair to your puppy to feed him in a busy environment where children or other pets may interfere with his eating. This can be the cause of food guarding. I always recommend that my puppies be fed in their crates where they do not feel threatened. Another advantage of this is that the puppy gets down to the business of eating and doesn't fool around.

Keeping your puppies entertained and occupied with toys, like this Gumabone® Frisbee™*, will help prevent them from getting into mischief. *The trademark Frisbee is used under license from Mattel Inc., CA, USA.

Perhaps you have seen possessiveness over the food bowl or his toys. Start by feeding him out of your hand and teach him that it is okay for you to remove his food bowl or toy and that you most assuredly will return it to him. If your dog is truly a bad actor and intimidates you, try keeping him on leash and perhaps sit next to him making happy talk. At feeding time make him work for his reward (his dinner) by doing some obedience command such as sit or down.

Food guarding can be a sign of dominant behavior in your dog. Discourage this by feeding him in an area where he will not be distracted from his meal.

If your allow your Springer to develop bad habits, like lying on the couch, they can be very hard to break.

Before your problem gets out of control you should get professional help. If he is out of control over toys, perhaps you should dispose of them or at least put them away when young children are around.

Mischief and Misbehavior

All puppies and even some adult dogs will get into mischief at some time in their lives. You should start by "puppy proofing" your house. Even so it is impossible to have a sterile environment. For instance, if you would be down to four walls and a floor your dog could still chew a hole in the wall. What do you do? Remember puppies should never be left unsupervised so let us go on to the trusted adult dog that has misbehaved. His behavior may be an attention getter. Dogs, and even children, are known to do mischief even though they know they will be punished. Your puppy/dog will benefit from more attention and new direction. He may benefit from a training class or by reinforcing the obedience he has already learned. How about a daily walk? That could be a good outlet for your dog, time together and exercise for both of you.

Separation Anxiety

This occurs when dogs feel distress or apprehension when separated from their owners. One of the mistakes owners make is to set their dogs up for their departure.

If you must leave your puppy home alone, leave him in his crate. Your puppy will be protected and your belongings will be safe.

Do these look like the faces of mischief-makers? Even sweethearts like these can get into trouble if not closely supervised.

Some authorities recommend paying little attention to the pet for at least ten minutes before leaving and for the first ten minutes after you arrive home. The dog isn't cued to the fact you are leaving and if you keep it lowkey they learn to accept it as a normal everyday occurrence. Those dogs that are used to being crated usually accept your departure. Dogs that are anxious may have a serious problem and wreak havoc on the house within a few minutes after your departure. You can try to acclimate your dog to the separation by leaving for just a few minutes at a time, returning and rewarding him with a treat. Don't get too carried away. Plan on this process taking a long time. A behaviorist can set down a schedule for you. Those dogs that are insecure, such as ones obtained from a humane shelter or those that have changed homes, present more of a problem.

Punishment

A puppy should learn that correction is sometimes necessary and should not question your authority. An older dog that has never received correction may retaliate. In my opinion there will be a time for physical punishment but this does not mean hitting the dog. Do not use newspapers, fly swatters, etc. One type of correction, that is used by the mother dog when she corrects her puppies, is to take the puppy by the scruff and shake him *gently*. For the older, larger dog you can grab the scruff, one hand on each side of his neck, and lift his legs off the ground. This is effective since dogs feel intimidated when their feet are off the ground. Timing is of the utmost importance when punishment is necessary. Depending on the degree of fault, you might want to reinforce punishment by ignoring your dog for 15 to 20 minutes. Whatever you do, do not overdo corrections or they will lose value.

My most important advice to you is to be aware of your dog's actions. Even so, remember dogs are dogs and will behave as such even though we might like them to be perfect little people. You and your dog will become neurotic if you worry about every little indiscretion. When there is reason for concern—don't waste time. Seek guidance. Dogs are meant to be loved and enjoyed.

References:

Manual of Canine Behavior, Valerie O'Farrell, British Small Animal Veterinary Association.

Good Owners, Great Dogs, Brian Kilcommons, Warner Books.

Your Springer is happiest when being loved and enjoyed by his owner. Author Art Perle with his friend Glen Robin Tee Dude.

SUGGESTED READING

TS-214
*Skin & Coat Care For
Your Dog
432 pages, over 300
full-color photos*

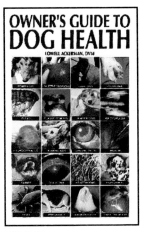

TS-249
*Owner's Guide to Dog
Health
224 pages, over 190
full-color photos*

TS-252
*Dog Behavior and Training
292 pages, over 200 full-
color photos*

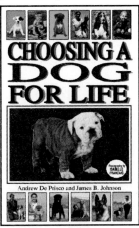

TS-257
*Choosing A Dog for Life
384 pages, over 700
full-color photos*

INDEX